LEO KERSLEY AND JANET SINCLAIR
DRAWINGS BY PETER REVITT

A DICTIONARY OF
BALLET TERMS

A DA CAPO PAPERBACK

Library of Congress Cataloging in Publication Data

Kersley, Leo.
   A dictionary of ballet terms.

   Reprint of the 3d rev. ed. published by A. & C.
Black, London.
   Includes index.
   1. Ballet — Dictionaries. 2. Dancing — Dictionaries.
I. Sinclair, Janet, joint author. II. Title.
GV1585.K45   1979   792.8'2'03   78-27421
ISBN 0-306-80094-2

For

BILL

whose idea this was

with love from
all three of us

ISBN 0-306-80094-2

This Da Capo Press paperback edition of *A Dictionary of
Ballet Terms* is an unabridged republication of the third revised
edition published by Adam and Charles Black in London in 1977.
It is reprinted with the permission of the authors.

Published by Da Capo Press, Inc.
A Subsidiary of Plenum Publishing Corporation
233 Spring Street, New York, New York 10013

INTRODUCTION TO THE THIRD EDITION

Ballet nomenclature is a maze through which even the most experienced of dancers is forced to move warily, and the wider his experience the more complicated the matter becomes, for there are in existence today almost so many branches and variations of the different schools of ballet technique as there are different churches in the Christian religion: one step or a single position of the arms may be accorded five or six different designations, in addition to the method of the majority of teachers who simply say "Like this," and demonstrate what they require. (Incidentally, this latter is the way in which most choreographers work, too : future would-be professionals kindly note.) This sort of casual attitude is obviously the result of a technique which depends on word of mouth and on eye : textbooks have indeed been written but remarkably few ballet students take the trouble to read any but their own particular gospel (if that) and the best of them are riddled with omissions and inaccuracies of description.

In addition, matters can be seriously complicated by the fact that ballet terminology is 99 per cent in French, and that 99 per cent of the English (or American or Russian or Chinese) students and teachers employing it do not speak or understand that language, so merely use a series of unusual sounds, like a parrot repeating "Pretty Polly," to which sounds after long practice the student may succeed in attaching a corresponding movement (see *Fondu*, pp. 65–66). If the student possesses a smattering of French his situation can be worse, for having realised that "*sissonne—fermé*" means to jump from both feet into the air, land on one foot, and after landing close the other foot down, he then takes this step to be a "closed *sissonne*" and can spend no end of time wondering vaguely what an open *sissonne* (*sissonne ouverte*) could be ; whereas in fact the phrase "*sissonne fermé*" means "perform a *sissonne*, and then, when it is completed, close the feet together." (Of course, he may be bedevilled at the same time by hearing a *sissonne* referred to as a "*jeté* from two feet"—simply because many teachers insist that every step begins from "the fifth position"—but this is taking matters too far for the lay reader.)

How much more frustrating yet, then, is the case of that innocent and untrained member of the ballet audience who would like to use the correct term instead of such phases as "That bit, *you* know, when Odile stands on one leg and flaps the other one and whizzes round and round", or "That part when the Blue Boy sort of leans his shoulders down to the stage and flips his legs up at the back one after the other all round the stage in a big circle." It was to attempt to give such a person some sort of basis of technical vocabulary that this book was

3

originally published in 1952, and also with the idea that the ballet-lover would find his appreciation of technical points heightened by having some idea of where to look for what step in which ballet. Unfortunately during the past twenty years the ballet world has developed more and more cannibalistic tendencies and today few of the classical ballets survive in anything remotely resembling their original form, and it is a sobering thought, or should be, that in fifty years' time not one single example from the several hundred given in this book may exist any longer in the sections of the various ballets quoted in the text.

Though we intended the book for the lay reader, comments we have received since its publication force us to the conclusion that one or two dancers do read it : a well-known authority in the field of dance notation told us that, not being a dancer himself, he takes it with him when lecturing just to check that the technical term he is using in fact means what both he and his audience are intending it to mean : and a famous dancer-critic team acknowledged its use in the preparation of their textbook : so we have been encouraged to include such new items as the note (pp. 9–10) on the differentiation between *arabesque* and *quatrième derrière*, the entries on Rosin, Mirror Dancer, and the last paragraph on Achilles Tendon which are primarily of interest to professional dancers, though possibly members of the audience may find them interesting too. We were very sorry indeed that, despite much thought, we were unable to devise any way of including such pearls of wisdom as Dame Marie Rambert's prime requisite for success as a dancer ("200 per cent good health!") or Dame Ninette de Valois' statement that ten is the best age to begin ballet training ; or of suggesting that one of the best reasons—a major one—for the pre-eminence of Commonwealth dancers at the present time is the fact that such students are free of that blight of the profession, the " ballet mother " ; or of pointing out that dancers' occupational disease—bunions—would be eliminated if ballet shoemakers were encouraged to make left and right shoes, instead of both feet the same as in the days of Henry VIII.

Finally, we hope that if there should be yet another edition of this Dictionary in another twenty years' time or so, we shall by then be able to include a valid definition of " National Ballet." At present the word is employed after the manner of Humpty Dumpty and means exactly what it is told. For though a National Ballet would seem by definition to mean a company of the highest possible standard, entirely State-supported and existing to preserve masterpieces of the past in pristine condition side by side with contemporary creations ; an organisation in which the dancer, once accepted, can feel safe for life with a pension at the end of his brief career and can therefore feel free to concentrate on art and not on string-pulling ; yet in practice it is simply a name.

appropriated by an astute management, serving the purpose only of any other name in differentiating the company in the eyes of the public from other companies with other less or more pretentious names. This odd state of affairs, if not existing in France, Denmark or Russia, is clearly to be seen in Holland, America, England and Canada, where dancers have no more security than they ever had and where commercial considerations reign supreme.

We must add our thanks to all those who have helped us, made suggestions and corrections, and demonstrated obscure steps, but as this list now runs literally from Alonso to Zullig we are reduced, through reasons of space, to thanking all our many helpful friends collectively, and saying once again that any corrections or emendations will be most gratefully received by

Leo Kersley and Janet Sinclair

Harlow, Essex.

NOTE. The following items omitted in 1964 for lack of space and for reasons of printing economy, are included here now.

GUEST ARTIST, PERMANENT

The meaning of this seemingly contradictory title has been clarified by the statement that " a permanent guest artist is a dancer who appears when he or she wishes, in rôles which he or she chooses." It might be pertinent to add to this classification the words " and for whose performance the Management raises the prices of admission, thereby obtaining a larger Government subsidy."

There might be some sense in this title if it were used to differentiate the guest artist from the permanent member of the company in the case of the former being employed only from year to year and not being eligible for pension. However, as " permanent " members of English companies also are only employed on yearly contracts and do not receive pensions on retirement from dancing, there is no such differentiation and the average person's bewilderment when faced with such a title is understandable.

KIT or POCHETTE

In the eighteenth century, a pocket-sized round-backed string instrument (kit) with which dancing masters accompanied their lessons. In the 19th century this was superseded by a miniature violin (pochette), which was still in use in St. Petersburg 1903, as one can see from the famous caricature of Christian Johanssen by Nicholas Legat. Rehearsals of the original " Swan Lake " in Moscow less than a century ago (1878) were accompanied by two violin players.

FOR reasons of uniformity, it should be assumed that all steps commence from the fifth position of the feet, the right foot in front (p. 64, Figure 78), unless the step cannot be performed in a series from that position. Obviously all steps can equally well be performed in the reverse fashion.

Throughout the text, when a leg is described as " extended " it should be understood that the feet are not together, but that one leg is raised with the foot either touching the floor or held in mid-air.

(*N.B.* This use of the word in the text should not be confused with the balletic use of this word, see p. 77.)

ABSTRACT BALLET. See also DIVERTISSEMENT

A term first mentioned in connection with Massine's " Ode " (1928) in which Diaghileff attempted to put the vogue of abstract painting, then a novelty, on to the stage. An abstract ballet is one in which the dancers appear as figures in a pattern and only mark cerebral relationship, without creation of mood or character. Ashton's " Scènes de Ballet " is a particularly happy example.

ACHILLES TENDON

The term " Achilles heel " is so frequently used metaphorically that it can easily be forgotten that the Achilles tendon for the dancer really is the most vulnerable part of the body, in no less degree than it was for the Greek hero. Dancers can survive accidents to almost every portion of their anatomy, sometimes in a way which baffles their doctors, but we have yet to encounter a dancer who has survived a major tear in the Achilles tendon, although it is possible nowadays to operate for this, and those who have damaged it only slightly have to take extra care throughout their careers.

Since the prime object of the *demi-plié* is to ensure that the Achilles tendon is supple, pliant and in good working order, and since almost every movement in classical ballet begins and ends in this position (involving either one leg or both), it will be immediately understood why every classical ballet class begins with *pliés*, and why all professional dancers will not fail to " do some *pliés* " before rehearsal or performance.

Upon the *demi-plié* depends the dancer's ability to jump (since the further down he can go, the higher he can throw himself into the air) and to land steadily. It is generally acknowledged that the Russian girls have higher, wider and softer jumps than Western dancers and possibly this comes partly from the fact that they do not in private life affect the ridiculous high heels which are accepted in the West as a necessary ingredient of the *chic* woman's wardrobe ; some stupid members of the audience laughed at the flat-heeled " childish " shoes worn by the Bolshoi dancers, but this type of footwear does not produce bunched, bulging calves and shorten the Achilles tendon as do the high heels of contemporary Western fashions.

ACROBAT. See also ADAGIO

Derogatory term applied to the virtuoso dancer who is not concerned with dancing as a whole, but merely with performing the largest possible number of pirouettes, or forcing her legs still higher into the air irrespective of distortion in the hip-line, etc.

ADAGE, ADAGIO

1. The opening section of the conventional *pas de deux*, that is, adagio and/or *entrée*, Variation I, Variation II, Coda. These terms can bear some relation, or none at all, to their musical equivalents. For example, the adagio from the *pas de deux* known as " The Black Swan " from " Swan Lake " is described on the score as " tempo de valse ma non troppo vivo quasi moderato " ; this is followed by a solo for the Prince, Variation I, which is unrelated to the previous music and was composed later by another musician (Drigo or Kadletz); while the next solo, Variation II for Odile, is an orchestration made after Tchaikowsky's death of a piece for piano. The Coda is an independent piece of music bearing no relation to what has gone before, unlike its equivalent in the world of music. 2. Partnering, also known as *pas de deux* or double work, when the man aids his partner's elegance, lightness and turning ability by holding, lifting and steadying her. 3. Section of a ballet named after the music. 4. Part of a ballet lesson, and the steps in that section (p. 41).

(*N.B. Adagio* is more commonly used to describe the work of acrobatic dancers.)

AILES DE PIGEON. See PISTOLET

AIR, EN L'

1. A position of the leg (p. 77, Figure 110). 2. A movement thus qualified is performed with the relevant leg raised from the ground. 3. A step performed while jumping (see also SAUTÉ).

ALLEGRO

1. Part of a ballet class (p. 42) and the steps contained therein. 2. Definition of part of a ballet by reference to the music.

ALLONGÉ. See also ARABESQUE; ATTITUDE; TOUR EN L'AIR
An almost horizontal pose.

ANGE, SAUT DE L'

The dancer springs off both feet and jumps forwards or backwards, with both legs straight and clinging together, inclining the
whole body in the direction in which he is travelling and landing
on both feet. The obliqueness of the body in the air is the only
differentiation between this step and an ordinary *soubresaut.*

ANGE, TEMPS DE L' or *TEMPS PLANÉ*

Resembles a SOUBRESAUT POISSON but the knees are bent.

APLOMB. See ÉQUILIBRE

ARABESQUE. See also p. 12, Figures 6, 8 ; LEGS, POSITIONS OF THE ; CHASSÉ ; TURN OUT

One leg is extended behind the dancer with straight knee and
pointed foot, the supporting leg either bent or straight. The body
is held erect.

In *arabesque* ALLONGÉE the line of the body is roughly parallel
to the floor.

In *arabesque* PENCHÉE the dancer leans down to the ground to
form a line inclining downwards from the raised back foot to the
outstretched hand or hands. This line may also be produced
when the dancer's arms are extended behind her.

To perform *arabesque penchée* the dancer usually stands on a
straight leg in *arabesque* and then leans forward and back again
in a slow see-saw movement, keeping the body and raised leg in
fixed alignment. (*N.B.* Nothing is more ugly than the spectacle
of a dancer lifting her back leg as far as she can and then continuing to stretch arm and shoulders further down to the floor.)

In *arabesque* and *arabesque allongée* the back foot may rest on
the ground (POINTE TENDUE).

On her entry in the " Blue Bird " pas de deux *the ballerina executes
an* arabesque *with the body erect* (*Figure* 1).

Before Giselle begins to dance in Act 2 (*see* PIROUETTES, SAUTÉS)
her bow to Mythra forms an arabesque allongée *with the right foot*
pointe tendue (*Figure* 3).

In Act 2 of " Coppélia " as Swanilda takes the mirror from Dr.
Coppelius she steps into an arabesque allongée, *slowly revolves once*
(PROMENADE) *and then performs* arabesque penchée (*Figure* 2).

FIGURE 1

FIGURE 2

FIGURE 3

Arabesques can easily be defined first by the relationship of the legs to the audience (CROISÉ and ÉFFACÉ), secondly by the relationship of arms and legs (OPPOSITION or OUVERTE), but many systems now number them in an almost infinite variety of ways.

(*N.B.* Cecchetti differentiates between *arabesque* and QUATRI-ÈME DERRIÈRE by using the former term for a pose and the latter for the position when used in the course of a movement.

9

This is logical, since when performing a high *arabesque* (*Figure 2*) the dancer cannot get her leg straight up so far behind herself unless she turns the front leg and twists her hips sideways, resulting in a kind of second position : however, if she were to attempt to do this in the course of sequences of steps such as JETÉS PASSÉS EN ARRIÈRE, the resultant swinging of the hips from side to side would make the movement slow, clumsy and almost impossible of execution. It is important therefore that the dancer when practising at the barre should keep the hips steady and never let GRANDS BATTEMENTS *en quatrième derrière* become *grands battements en arabesque*. Dancers often use one or other of these terms to the exclusion of the other, but it is valuable to the student to be made aware of the difference.)

ARMS, POSITIONS OF THE. See pp. 12–13

ARQUÉ. See also METHOD

It is a common fallacy to-day that the most beautiful legs are perfectly straight: hence the detrimental use of the terms bow-legged (*arqué*, p. 64, Figure 80) and knock-kneed (JARRETÉ). However, the study of anatomy will quickly convince one that Noverre's division of the adult human physique into these two categories is correct, as absolutely straight legs are so rare as to require no special term.

Generally children are very knock-kneed, but if they become powerful and tightly-knit as adults the muscles of the leg will make the bones set so that when the feet are together and parallel a gap is seen between the knees. This is not a malformation to be remedied, any more than is its opposite; but merely evidence of a powerful physique, common among boxers and sprinters, possessing certain advantages and drawbacks which it is futile to attempt to alter.

The *arqué* dancer is remarkable for her power and *ballon*, and best expresses herself in movement, not in pose. Because she is tightly knit her extensions are never very high; loosening and stretching exercises only lessen her natural abilities and make her a straining copy of the *jarreté* type of dancer, who is remarkable for the elegant clarity of her movement and the beauty of her positions. This difference in physique is as great as the vocal difference between a soprano and a contralto: the singing teacher who attempted to make all his students sing in the same register irrespective of voice would find few pupils, yet this is continually attempted in the ballet world though it would be more sensible to make the most of the contrast.

ARRIÈRE, EN. See p. 52

ARRONDI. See p. 13

ARTIST. See also PERMANENT GUEST ARTIST (p. 5)

The Oxford English Dictionary definition of " artist " includes the words " one who makes his craft a fine art." The distinction between craftsmen and artists is applicable to dancers; for the expert craftsman of the dance may not have the intellectual approach by which to transform his craft into fine art, nor may he be interested in so doing.

There is a vast difference between the dancer who treats technique as an end in itself, and the dancer who uses his or her technical equipment, such as it may be, with artistry: for instance, the dancer who controls her movements to make them uniformly soft, or clear and precise throughout, or to give each step its own different character: or the dancer who phrases his steps to underline either the musical phrase or their dramatic character. There are infinite ways in which dancers can show artistry, and when labelling a dancer " a great artist " some qualification of the statement is necessary.

ASSEMBLÉ. See also FERMÉ

A firm step ending on both feet.

1. The dancer throws one leg up and springs off the other: while ascending the raised leg continues to rise. On landing, both feet close down together. When performed with a slight spring, an *assemblé* is usually a preparatory movement: however, it is effective in itself when performed with a high spring. *Assemblé* can travel in the direction in which the leg was raised, and can be performed while turning, or with a beat.

Small travelling beaten *assemblés* are called BRISÉS.

2. *Assemblé* SUR LES POINTES (not a jump). The dancer brings one foot in sharply as she springs on to her toes, with the legs close together. This is usually performed turning, when the dancer makes a bold sweep of the leg round to the front or the back before swivelling round with the feet close together (DÉTOURNÉ). *Assemblé sur les pointes* is often performed with a slight stop (SOUTENU) at the end.

In the second diagonal of his solo, the male dancer of the " Blue Bird " pas de deux *performs a series of three alternating* SOU-BRESAUTS POISSON (p. 101, *Figure* 123) *and* assemblés de côté battus p. 14, *Figure* 22), *sometimes called* ENTRECHAT DE VOLÉ.

FIGURE 4.
Fifth (Mme. Legat).

FIGURE 5.
Demi-Bras (French Method,
Lawson, Espinosa, former R.A.D.).
Demi-Second (Cecchetti, R.A.D.).

FIGURE 6.
Arabesque à Deux Bras
(Espinosa, former R.A.D.).
Third Arabesque (Cecchetti,
R.A.D.).

FIGURE 7.
Bras Adorés (French
Method)

FIGURE 8.
Arabesque (French Method).
Arabesque Ouverte
(Espinosa).
First Arabesque (R.A.D.).

FIGURE 9.
Bras en Avant (French
Method).
The Gateway (Espinosa,
former R.A.D.).
First (Lifar, R.A.D., Lawson,
Karsavina, Vaganova).
Second (Mme. Legat).
Fifth en Avant (Cecchetti).

FIGURE 10.
Bras En Répos (French
Method).
First (Cecchetti, Kniaseff).

FIGURE 11.
Bras Bas (R.A.D.).
Preparatory (Vaganova,
Lawson).
First (Mme. Legat).
Fifth en Bas (Cecchetti).
Seventh (Lifar).

FIGURE 12.
Opposition en Bas (French
Method).
Third (Cecchetti).
Low Third (R.A.D.).

Cecchetti's positions of ONE arm are illustrated by either arm in Figure 10 which equals 1st,
Figure 16 which equals 2nd, Figure 5 which equals 3rd, Figure 19 which equals 4th *en haut*,
Figure 9 which equals 4th *en avant*, Figure 4 which equals 4th *en arrière*, Figure 11 which
equals 5th.

FIGURE 13.
Attitude Grecque (French Method).
Fourth (former R.A.D.).
Low Fourth (R.A.D.).

FIGURE 14.
Third (former R.A.D.).

FIGURE 15.
Croisé attitude (French Method).
Attitude (Cecchetti).

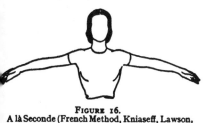

FIGURE 16.
A là Seconde (French Method, Kniaseff, Lawson, Cecchetti, Espinosa, Lifar, R.A.D.).
First (former R.A.D.).
Fourth (Mme. Legat).

FIGURE 17.
Bras en Lyre(French Method).

FIGURE 18.
Bras Croisé (French Method).
Bras Croisé (Espinosa, former R.A.D.).
Third (R.A.D.).
Fourth en Avant (Cecchetti)
Sixth (Lifar).

FIGURE 19.
Bras en Couronne (French Method).
À Deux Bras (Espinosa).
Attitude à Deux Bras (former R.A.D.).
Third (Mme. Legat, Lawson, Kniaseff, Vaganova).
Fifth (Lifar, R.A.D.).
Fifth en Haut (Cecchetti).

FIGURE 20.
Fourth (Lifar).
Fourth Crossed (R.A.D.).

FIGURE 21.
Bras en Attitude (French Method).
Attitude Ordinaire or Opposition (Espinosa).
Second (former R.A.D.).
Third (Lifar).
Fourth (R.A.D.)
Fourth en Haut (Cecchetti).

When arms normally held in a rounded position are extended, the pose is said to be EXTENDED in the reverse case, the term used is ARRONDI. See p. 9, Figure 1; for an example of *bra en couronne* (Figure 19) extended.

13

──── Figure 22

À TERRE. See TERRE

ATTACK, ATTAQUE

A dancer who performs steps or *enchaînements* in a very clear, incisive and definite manner is said to have attack.

ATTITUDE. See also p. 13, Figures 13, 15, 19, 21 ; LEG, POSITIONS OF THE (Figure 104)

One leg is bent either behind the dancer or in front (*attitude* DEVANT); the supporting leg is either bent or straight. *Attitudes* like *arabesques* can be POINTE TENDUE, ALLONGÉE, or PENCHÉE.

In Italian-trained dancers the raised foot is always held below the raised knee, whereas with Russian training it can be held above (so that greater height is attained); many examples of this type of attitude can be seen in the performance of Soviet dancers.

This differentiation arose from the fact that most of the strongly-built Italian virtuosi of the 19th century had bow-legs, while the Russian dancers (with their inclination towards elegance) tended to be knock-kneed. As a consequence of the natural construction of these two types of legs, the foot of the Italian dancer when he bent his knee in attitude fell automatically below knee-height, while the reverse was the case for the Russians.

FIGURE 23

In the Nocturne in " Les Sylphides," immediately after the first entrance of the Waltz dancer, she, the Mazurka dancer and the male dancer form a group in the middle of the stage in which both the girls are in attitude devant *supported by the man (Figure 23).*

*At the end of the Rose Adage in Act 1 of " The Sleeping Beauty," Aurora is slowly turned round on place (*PROMENADE*) in* attitude *by each of her four suitors (p. 62, Figure 72).*

(*N.B.* In some contemporary ballets, notably Tudor's, the dancer holds her leg bent at the side (*attitude* DE CÔTÉ.)

AUTOUR DE LA SALLE. See MANÈGE, EN

AVANT, EN, See p. 52

BACK BEND. See CAMBRÉ

BAISSÉ

1. The dancer standing on point or half-point lowers the heel or heels to the ground. 2. The male dancer lowers his partner to the stage after a lift. 3. The dancer leans forward (also called PENCHÉ).

15

BALANCÉ

FIGURE 24

A rocking step in waltz rhythm. The dancer stands on his right leg, the ball of the left foot lightly touching the ground behind. He steps out to the side on the left foot, bringing the right behind it with the ball on the floor: next he takes the weight for a moment on the right foot, which does not change position. Finally he transfers the weight firmly back to the left foot, and is ready to reverse the step if required. This can also be performed with the leg crossing in front of the other.

Balancé can also be done swaying backwards and forwards instead of from side to side, with the foot first taken to front or back instead of to the side.

In the finale of "Les Sylphides" when the man rejoins his partner after his short solo they do balancé en avant *and* en arrière *facing each other before the girl is lifted, then two more* balancés *back to back (Figure 24), and a lift, before repeating the first sequence.*

BALANÇOIRE, BATTEMENT. See CLASS (p. 38)

BALLABILE (Italian)

A group dance, usually for *corps de ballet*, without solos.

BALLERINA, PRIMA (Italian), (masculine *PRIMO BALLERINO*, obsolete outside Italy)

In the days of the Imperial Russian Ballet this title was given to the outstanding female soloist or soloists dancing the leading classical roles. There was only one higher rank, Prima Ballerina Assoluta, held by only two ballerinas in two hundred years. After Diaghileff formed his own company in Paris and ballet broke away from the confines of the Opera House to enter upon a nomad phase of existence, the use of the term prima ballerina became more loose until to-day the title is applied to any leading dancer, regardless of her qualifications.

In Paris, where the old system of rank persists, dancers bear formal titles as follows : *premières danseuses étoiles/premiers danseurs étoiles, premières danseuses/premiers danseurs, grands sujets, mimes, petits sujets, coryphées, premiers quadrilles, deuxièmes quadrilles.* Children appearing in performances are called *élèves* or *rats.* (*N.B.* The literal translation of ballerina is dancer.)

BALLERINES PRÈS DE L'EAU

A slang term used to describe the oldest and most unsuccessful members of the *corps de ballet* of the Paris Opera in the 19th century. The term arose because the conventional backcloth of the period usually had a fountain painted on it (as in Hugh Stevenson's design for " Gala Performance," Scene 2) : therefore the back row of the *corps de ballet* became known as the ballerinas near the water.

BALLET

A theatrical work in which a choreographer, assisted by music, décor and lighting, attempts to express his ideas in movement: he might be considered a painter using moving figures. The choreographer can tell a story, create a mood, string a set of dances together, or use his dancers as units in an abstract scheme; if he remembers Noverre's dictum " ballet is a sort of machine " and makes the work logical within itself, it should be convincing, particularly if he is fertile in the invention of dancing sequences (ENCHAÎNEMENTS).

Ashton has extraordinary command of balletic language; in all his ballets it is the quality of the movement which is outstanding, whereas the ballets of Tudor, Ashton's colleague at the Ballet Club in the early 'thirties, are remarkable for their unusual subjects and clever construction. The best ballets of Fokine and

Jooss are at once convincingly constructed, and contain movements which would be enjoyable if divorced from their context. This was possibly true of the ballets of Noverre and Viganò.

Leonide Massine said in the course of a lecture given in Holland a few years ago, while enthusing about Fokine's work, that the only reason for making a new ballet was because one had something new to say, or at least an entirely new manner of saying it. These words from one (with Fokine) of the two most creative choreographers of this century—indeed, arguably the two most creative choreographers the world has ever known—are worthy of note since if they were followed the number of new ballets presented would be dramatically cut, and the critic would not have to scratch his head weekly in order to think of something to say about ballets which, to quote Noverre, are " no more than pale copies of the copies which have preceded them."

BALLET BLANC

This term is applied to any ballet performed in the traditional long white skirt said to have been invented by Lami for Taglioni in " La Sylphide," for example " Les Sylphides " or " Giselle " Act 2, and is generally synonymous with the idea of ballet held by the person who has little experience of ballet. (It is held by some authorities, cited by Lifar, that Lami's skirt was in fact light blue in colour.)

BALLET CLASSIQUE. See CLASSICAL BALLET

BALLET D'ACTION or NARRATIVE BALLET. See also CLASSICAL BALLET

A ballet in which the mainspring of the conception is the plot and characters, for example " Petrouchka," " The Rake's Progress," " The Witch Boy," " The Invitation " and " Romeo and Juliet ".

BALLET D'ÉCOLE

Ballet in which the accent is on the dancing, which is performed as in ballet class, with legs turned out, arms rounded, etc.

BALLET MASTER or MISTRESS. See MAÎTRE DE BALLET

BALLETOMANE, BALLETOMANIA

A balletomane is a person with a mania for ballet: the word was invented in Russia in the early 19th century.

BALLET, ROMANTIC. See CLASSICAL BALLET
BALLON

A quality of movement by which the impression is given that the dancer, by a reversal of the laws of gravity, is continuously thrown off the ground, instead of pushing himself away from it, and should not be confused with ELEVATION, which is more concerned with the height of the dancer's jumps.

Ballon is remarkable in the jumps of Wayne Sleep.

BALLONNÉ

A *ballonné* always ends (and usually begins) with one foot touching the other leg, either the knee (GRAND *ballonné*) or the ankle (PETIT or SIMPLE). The dancer springs, at the same time extending the bent leg loosely from the knee to front, side or back, and returning it on landing (Figure 25); the step may be performed travelling in the direction of the raised foot. This movement can also be performed rising on to the supporting toe instead of jumping.

BRISÉS BALLONNÉS or BALLONNÉS BATTUS are only done to the side, and the raised foot always touches the other ankle, never the knee. The dancer beats the supporting leg beneath the other at the height of the jump.

The main difference between a *ballonné* and a PETIT FOUETTÉ SAUTÉ (see illustration p. 5) is that in the first the accent is out and up, on the second it is in and down.

Giselle opens the first dance she performs with the corps de ballet *on the stage with three* ballonnés PORTÉS EN AVANT, *and a* PAS DE BASQUE EN AVANT SAUTÉ, *which sequence she performs three times on alternating feet. Later she performs it with Albrecht. (Figure* 25.) (For another example see BALLOTTÉ.)

FIGURE 25

19

BALLOTTÉ or *JETÉ BALLOTTÉ* or *JETÉ BATEAU* or *DÉVELOPPÉ PASSÉ SAUTÉ*

Ballotté consists of a COUPÉ (usually jumped) and a DÉVELOPPÉ. Standing on the right leg, the left extended behind him, the dancer springs from the supporting leg, bending both legs up beneath him in mid-air. On descending he lowers the left foot to the ground and extends the right foot in front. He springs up again, bringing both feet beneath him as before, landing on the right leg and placing the left behind him. These two steps are usually performed in a series, creating a swaying movement: hence the name occasionally used for this step of JETÉ BATEAU. This step can be performed with the dancer's legs straight, not bent, beneath him during the jump, in which case the dancer may add beats.

FIGURE 26

Immediately after the flower episode in the opening scene of " Giselle," Giselle and Albrecht do four ballottés *(front (Figure 26), back, front, back) and then a* BALLONNÉ *(Figure 25) to the side, a step, and a* GRAND JETÉ *in front. They then repeat the whole sequence to the other side.*

BAREFOOT DANCE. See FREE DANCE

BARRE. See CLASS; WARMING UP

BAS, EN. See p. 12, Figures 11, 12

BASQUE, PAS DE

A step in three movements, somewhat reminiscent of the basic waltz step (forward, side, together) in ballroom dancing. The dancer sweeps the right foot to the front, then out to the side: next she springs on to it, and slides the left foot past to the front, when the right foot (now at the back) stretches and closes behind the left. A turn may be added on the left foot as the right foot closes. The step can also be done backwards, beginning with the left foot swinging out to the back or side.

If the step glides and the spring is slight, the *pas de basque* is GLISSÉ; if the first movement is made with a high jump and sweep, it is SAUTÉ.

For example see BALLONNÉ.

BASQUE, GRAND PAS DE. See also PASSÉ

The dancer throws the front leg forward and springs, immediately throwing the supporting leg forward as well, so that it rises as the other descends and then closes in front. This may end with the legs crossed so that the dancer may swivel round (DÉTOURNÉ) on the toes, when the words EN TOURNANT are added.

When the Sugar Plum Fairy in her solo travels forward diagonally from the audience's left, she performs a grand pas basque (*Figure* 27), *two steps, another* grand pas de basque *and a series of little* PAS DE BOURRÉE *on the spot before repeating the whole sequence.*

At the end of her solo in the "Black Swan" pas de deux, Odile performs a series of petits grands pas de basque en tournant *while travelling round the stage* (EN MANÈGE).

BASQUE, SAUT DE or JETÉ DEVANT EN TOUR- NANT. See also JETÉ ENVELLOPPÉ

The dancer takes a preparatory step on his right foot in the direction of the front right hand corner of the stage, bending both knees. He then throws his left leg up before him to the corner, and jumps in that direction into a vertical position, the left leg beneath him and the right foot drawn up to the left knee or ankle. In this position he describes a turn to the right in the air, landing to face front in that position. He is then ready to step out in the same direction if necessary. A big or small jump may be used.

When the man enters in the coda of the "Peasant" pas de deux from "Giselle," both dancers moving in opposite directions perform two big sauts de basque *crossing the stage, then a step forward, a little* cabriole *in front and then a* JETÉ *forward, before repeating this sequence each in the reverse direction.*

FIGURE 27   FIGURE 28

Because of its extreme difficulty, a saut de basque turning twice in the air is rarely used, but Balanchine requires his ballerina to attempt it in the final movement of " Ballet Imperial " (Figure 28).

BATTEMENTS. See CLASS (p. 36—*grand* ; *tendu* ; *tendu jeté* ; *tendu glissé* ; *glissé* ; *degagé.* p. 37—*tendue relevé* ; *relevé.* p. 39—*frappé* ; *petit.* p. 40—*battu* ; *en cloche* ; *balançoire* ; *jeté balancé*)

BATTERIE. See BATTU, BRISÉ, CABRIOLE, ENTRECHAT
Term covering all jumping steps to which a beat has been added. The Danish dancers excel in *batterie*, as did those of the pure French school, of which the Bournonville tradition is the purest example surviving today.

BATTU. See also BEATS
This word added to the name of a step does not imply any alteration in the basic movement, but that the dancer beats his calves together during the movement, and possibly also changes the position of his legs while doing so.

For example see ASSEMBLÉ, ÉCHAPPÉ, FOUETTÉ.

22

BEATS

The dancer executes a beat in the course of a jumping step when he strikes both calves sharply together so that they rebound. The legs are then ready to beat again, to change places before beating again, or to continue the movement.

BLOCK SHOES or TOE SHOES. See POINTE

BODY, DIRECTIONS OF. See DIRECTIONS

BOURRÉE, PAS DE

1. *Pas de bourrée* CHAINÉ, nowadays known as *pas de bourrée* COURU, is a step in which the dancer appears to glide along on her toes, picking them up minutely in quick succession. This movement may also be performed on the spot, in which case the dancer may turn. Generally the feet are together in *pas de bourrée courus*, but many dancers in "Checkmate" perform *pas de bourrée courus* with the legs apart. Often girls prepare for a supported *pirouette* with the legs opening to front and back in *pas de bourrée courus*.
The sleepwalking scene in "Night Shadow" is composed of pas de bourrée chaînés *both travelling and turning.*

The Betrayed Girl makes her entrance in the third scene of "The Rake's Progress", when the Creditors are awaiting the Rake, in a

FIGURE 29

FIGURE 30

series of pas de bourrée courus *without turnout of the legs (Figure* 29).

In *her first entrance, Myrtha in Act* 2 *of " Giselle " glides diagonally across the stage in* pas de bourrée courus *(Figure* 30).

2. *Pas de bourrée* consists of three movements. The dancer (*a*) bends the left knee, the right leg extending just clear of the floor; then straightens the left leg and rises on the toe while the right moves in to join the left leg; (*b*) takes the weight on the right leg, and steps out on to the left toe in the opposite direction; (*c*) bends the left leg and closes the right in to it; the left foot may then rise to touch the right leg just clear of the floor.

As each foot leaves the floor, it may be picked up to the level of the other knee or ankle when the *pas de bourrée* is called PIQUÉ; *pas de bourrée* may also be performed while the dancer makes a turn, when a RENVERSÉ movement of the body may be added.

Odile precedes the thirty-two FOUETTÉS RONDS DE JAMBE EN TOURNANT *with a* pas de bourrée *turning* EN DEDANS.

3. *Pas de bourrée* OUVERTE, once called *pas de bourrée couru.* Unlike (2) above, this begins and ends with both feet apart. There is a lilting feeling about the movement, which is frequently used as a preparation for a jump. Standing with the feet apart the dancer bends the knees and brings the right foot in to replace the left, rising on to the toes. The left then steps out, continuing the direction of the movement, so that the dancer finishes with both heels on the ground again, ready to spring up into a jump (See BRISÉ).

4. *Pas de bourrée* FLEURET, a crablike movement.

While keeping the knees bent throughout the movement, the dancer shoots one foot out into second position and then closes the other foot in, immediately beginning again in the same direction. This movement slightly resembles *glissade* but the legs move in quick regular rhythm without the characteristic " breathing " rise and fall of glissades.

Danish dancers perform this movement superbly; particularly notable is Peter Schaufuss in "Flower Festival at Genzano" and it is used with startling effect when three dancers cross the stage, in a line behind one another, from wing to wing in " Danses Concertantes " (Macmillan). The step was a favourite with Kurt Jooss, who used it frequently, and perhaps most effectively of all in the opening and closing scenes of " The Big City " in which the relatively small *corps de ballet* gave an impression of tremendous complexity merely by travelling backwards and forwards across the stage in *pas de bourrée fleurets.*

BOW LEGS. See ARQUÉ

BRAS. See pp. 12–13, CLASS, *port de bras* (p. 41)

BRISÉ. See also BALLONNÉ

A small travelling *assemblé* with a beat, ending on both feet, in which the dancer uses her spring to skim across the floor, usually sideways. The dancer swings one foot to the side just clear of the floor and springs in that direction, quickly bringing the supporting leg to beat beneath the other, just off the floor, landing together.

Swanilda in Act 1 of " Coppélia " traverses the stage diagonally towards the audience doing eight brisés DESSUS *(Figure* 31*), and returns performing three* TEMPS LEVÉS EN ATTITUDE *on alternative feet, interspersed with* PAS DE BOURRÉE OUVERT. *She then takes a pose and repeats the* brisés.
N.B. "Danish" *brisés are jetés passés en avant battus* in a series with a *tombé* between each *jeté.*

FIGURE 31

BRISÉS VOLÉS or *SOUS DESSOUS SOUS DESSUS*

JETÉ PASSÉ BATTU preceded by a GRAND ROND DE JAMBE EN L'AIR at DÉGAGÉ height.
The dancer stands with the left foot extended behind. The left leg is swept in a slight arc to the front, when the dancer springs and brings the right leg up to beat beneath the left, which then descends to the ground leaving the right extended in front. He now sweeps the right leg round to the back and springs, beating it with the left, and landing on the right foot; and so on.
The coda of the " Blue Bird " pas de deux begins with a series of twenty-four brisés volés *alternately to the front and back. Babilée performs these* brisés volés *with a double beat.*

BROKEN WRISTS

A dancer who, even in classical rôles, breaks the line of her arm at the wrist by allowing the hand permanently to droop or bend back is said to have broken wrists. In the classroom most teachers will urge their pupils to avoid this since it distracts the spectator's eye from the rest of the movement, but like most faults to be avoided in class, it can be made use of on the stage to point the end of a solo or call attention to an individual. Fonteyn never breaks her arm line at the wrist in classical work: Ulanova did it frequently.

CABRIOLE or TEMPS LEVÉ BATTU. See also
FOUETTÉ (p. 68) ; ZÉPHYR, PAS DE

With one leg raised, the dancer springs from the supporting leg, which rises to beat beneath the raised leg. The dancer then lands on the supporting leg. The raised leg always maintains its position, to give the impression of a pose being held throughout the jump, and of the dancer being thrown higher in this position by the beat of the supporting leg. In fact the impact of the beat throws the raised leg a little higher, but once this movement becomes at all exaggerated the whole quality of a pose in the air is destroyed.

The *cabriole* is said to be *double* or *triple* when the calves beat twice or three times.

(*N.B.* In national dancing a *cabriole* to the side may be executed with bent legs, when only the soles beat, as in the Betrothal Dance in Act 3 of " Coppélia " (Figure 34). These *cabrioles* are also sometimes performed in ballet shoes.)

As Harlequin in " Carnaval" first jumps on to the stage he performs a double cabriole DEVANT (*Figure* 32).

The male dancer's solo in the finale of " Les Sylphides " consists of chassé coupé chassé, grand jetés en tournant dessus *in the centre of the stage and* cabrioles en arabesque (*Figure* 33) *to the wings.*

Immediately before the entry of the Prince in Ashton's " Cinderella," his four attendants, who are standing at the top of the steps, perform four cabrioles (*front, back, front, back*).

CAGNEAUX or KNOCK KNEES. See ARQUÉ

CAMBRÉ or AU CORPS CAMBRÉ
A bend of the body from the waist in any direction.

CARACTÈRE, AIR DE
Descriptive music used in ballets at the French court to depict the entry of the various characters.

FIGURE
32

FIGURE
33

FIGURE 34

CARRÉ, EN. See QUARRÉ, EN

CATEGORIES. See MOVEMENTS IN DANCING

CENTRAL EUROPIAN DANCE. See FREE DANCE

CENTRE PRACTICE. See CLASS (p. 41)

CHAINÉ. See BOURRÉE, PAS DE; TOURS, DEMI-

CHANGÉ and SANS CHANGER

    Terms used to qualify steps beginning and ending with the feet closed evenly together on the floor: i.e. TOURS EN L'AIR, ÉCHAPPÉ. If *changé* is added, the feet have changed places in the course of the step, and the foot originally at the back finishes in front and vice versa. If *sans changer* is used, the feet finish in their original position.

CHANGEMENTS DE PIEDS. See PIEDS, CHANGE-
    MENTS DE. *BATTUS.* See ENTRECHAT

CHARACTER DANCER: CHARACTER DANCING.
    See also CLASSICAL DANCER, DANSEUR NOBLE

Usually dancing based on folk or national dances. These may be either almost completely authentic, as in " Prince Igor," or may bear the slightest superficial resemblance to the dancing from which they are supposed to originate, as in the " Danse Chinoise " of " The Nutcracker " and the " Spanish Dance " in " Swan Lake ".

    Character dancing can also mean dancing based on the classical steps performed not for their own sake, but to express a clearly defined personality: for example a fencing-master's dance, or the dance of a suicide, or the dance of a wedding couple.

    The term " character dancer " has come to designate dancers who perform any of the above dances, and because of the wide field thus covered the term has become so loose as to mean almost anything. This lack of distinction between national dancing and dancing for the purpose of characterisation causes dancers who excel in one type of either to be thrust automatically into the others; this is occasionally successful, as the dancer with a flair for characterisation often has sufficient intelligence to make a good show in roles to which he may be unsuited: but it is by no means axiomatic that a dancer successful in one kind of national dancing will be suited to another kind—or that he will succeed in characterisation —because the physique suitable to one type is unsuitable to another.

Walter Camryn, who teaches in Chicago, has spent a considerable time studying various national dances and from them he has evolved a series of character classes designed to give students a thorough groundwork in the movements, rhythms and positions of national dancing which helps them begin to adapt their own movements to the many varied demands of characterisation which will be called for in a professional career. One feature of this class is the series of twenty basic foot movements defined by Camryn.

CHASSÉ. See also TEMPS LEVÉ CHASSÉ

1. The dancer slides a foot out in any direction, keeping the heel on the ground and bending that knee.
2. The dancer slides a foot out as in (1), bending both knees, in which case the dancer will continue the movement on to the sliding foot. (*N.B.* The former *chassé* resembles a lunge.)

At the opening of " Death and the Maiden " when Death and the Shadows have stepped into a line they all move downstage (see Rake of the Stage, p. 94) performing chassés.

Immediately after the pas de deux *in " Les Patineurs " the* corps de ballet *enter, four from either side, doing* chassé *(Figure 36) into* arabesque.

Chassé PASSÉ. The dancer arches one foot, passes it round the other ankle and executes a *chassé.*

CHAT, PAS DE or SAUT DE CHAT. See also JETÉ EN ATTITUDE (p. 75) and GARGOUILLADE

The dancer brings one foot up to the other knee or ankle and out a little as she springs, immediately bending the other leg beneath her and travelling sideways (see p. 71, Figure 96): she then closes the latter down after the former.

Towards the end of the dance of the four cygnets, in Act 2 of " Swan Lake " the dancers perform sixteen pas de chat *travelling diagonally forward* (p. 31, *Figure 37*).

CHAT, GRAND PAS DE or GRAND PAS DE CHAT JETÉ. See GRAND JETÉ EN AVANT (p. 72)

CHEVAL, PAS DE

The dancer hops on one foot while pawing the ground like a horse with the other.

In the coda of her solo in the " Don Quixote " pas de deux (Petipa-Oboukhoff), the dancer comes diagonally forward performing a series of two pas de cheval *on her toes on alternating feet (Figure 35).*

CHOREOGRAPHER, CHOREGRAPHER

At the beginning of the 18th century when this term was coined, it meant dance-notator; because such a person was usually also the creator of the dance (*maître de ballet*), the term came to cover both activities. As the art of dance notation vanished, the word choreographer assumed its current meaning of creator of dances, for which Lifar's suggested term " CHORÉAUTEUR " would seem more logical. (See also NOTATION.)

CHOREOGRAPHY, CHOREGRAPHY

The steps of a dance or ballet.

When the person to whom the choreography of a ballet is ascribed is dead or not at hand, it is unlikely, owing to the vagaries of ballet masters and the fallibility of dancers' memories, that the steps will remain as arranged: extra confusion is caused by many choreographers producing several versions of their works.

Ballets frequently change quite noticeably with the advent of a new ballet master; this would not happen so often or matter so much if the choreographers could still write their ballets down and it were therefore not so easy to tamper with them: then companies of the future could chose between the original or the " improvement," whereas to-day once a ballet is altered or dropped from the repertoire the original choreography is likely to disappear.

At the time when the first edition of this book was published in 1952, the practice of altering the choreography of 19th-century masterpieces right and left had only just begun to make itself manifest on our stages. True, Diaghilev had made certain changes in Fokine's " Firebird " which reduced the choreographer to a state of almost speechless indignation, and allowed new numbers by Nijinska to be inserted into Sergueeff's reproduction of " The Sleeping Princess " : but since we have Grigoriev's word for it that Fokine rehearsed " Giselle " for Diaghilev's Paris season in 1910 and Fokine's word for it that he never altered the works of previous masters, and since all that was done to " Le Lac des Cygnes " for Kchessinskaya's performances in London (1911) was a reduction to two acts " from its original three " (Grigoriev, p. 59), we can guess that these works at least had not been " improved " out of recognition. The remainder of the repertory was created or reproduced by choreographers to whose work—apart from the one instance of " Firebird " quoted above—Diaghilev would have been in no position to allow alterations.

Similarly in the case of the Ballets Russes of the thirties, the

FIGURE 35

FIGURE 36

FIGURE 37

choreographers directly responsible—Fokine, Massine and Balanchine—themselves mounted or supervised the remounting of their works, which ensured their authenticity : " Giselle " was mounted for Massine's Ballets Russes de Monte Carlo by Lifar, presumably reproducing the version extant at the Paris Opera since 1841, while Ninette de Valois at Sadler's Wells was engaging Sergueeff to reproduce (so far as possible with the available material) the 19th-century classics, of which his position as ballet master at St. Petersburg—at one time he had worked under Petipa himself—gave him ample knowledge.

Today, however, the position is radically altered, and it is ironical that just when the authenticity of the " Sergueeff versions " has been accepted through comparison with the Bolshoi " Giselle " and scraps of Soviet films made before the " improvement " craze swept in there too, these Sergueeff reproductions are all being swept away in a mad fury of alteration and re-creation which threaten to leave barely the bones of the original versions. It is hard to understand what prompts directors of ballet companies to allow (indeed, to encourage) choreographers to tinker with the works of masters of the past, for even apart from the waste of time involved (most of them would be better employed making new original works) once the original steps are gone from the stage, they are gone forever. One wonders what would be the reaction of the public and the critics if contemporary painters were invited to scrape out the face of the Mona Lisa and replace this with a portrait of Princess Margaret, or if contemporary musicians re-wrote the operas of Mozart, including the saxophone and smoothing away difficulties which contemporary singers have trouble in mastering, while at the same time burning every extant score and record of the original Mozart? (And even if such vandalism were permitted, we should not be so deprived as the ballet audience, for there are thousands of reproductions of the Mona Lisa in existence and thousands of gramophone records of " Don Giovanni.")

CISEAUX, PAS or *ÉCART EN L'AIR.*   See also
PASSÉ

The dancer springs and throws his feet wide apart (1) to either side; (2) to front and back (A LA QUATRIÈME) and closes on landing. *The male solo in " Les Rendezvous " begins with the dancer rising on his toes, followed by a pas ciseaux (Figure 38). He repeats this twice more and then performs several pirouettes. This sequence is then completely repeated.*

CLASS or LEÇON

FIGURE 38

It is the development of the ballet class which has transformed technique from a bunch of unrelated tricks to the scientific art it is to-day. Bad habits formed in his first years will haunt a dancer throughout his career: habits that he has suppressed for years in class will in his excitement return to upset him on the stage.

Class begins with BARRE work or SIDE PRACTICE, in which the dancer lightly rests one hand, well in front of him, on the bar which surrounds the classroom at about hip height. He must not clutch the bar, for if he is not perfectly calm and balanced now, what will happen later? He must also keep that hand, like the free one, in front of the body, because once the shoulder blades begin to lock an easy balance is destroyed and the weight is thrown backwards, the back arching. In the classroom, one must always keep the arms when extended to the side well before the chest line, so they may be taken back a little to counteract the rake of the stage when the dancer is performing. It is painful to see the straining shoulders of dancers battling with a rake when they have been trained to hold their arms out in one straight line with the shoulders.

The first exercise is PLIER in which the student slowly bends both knees as far as possible, keeping the bottom well in and only raising the heels when necessary, because this exercise is to stretch the muscles gently and to adjust the balance. Students who jerk down into a *plié* and raise the heels may one day do the same on concluding a difficult jump and tear the Achilles tendon. Others try complicated arm movements with *pliés*, destroying their balance and gripping the *barre* in attempting to regain it: therefore they lose coherence in jumping steps (see also PLIÉ).

In the Cecchetti system, GRANDS BATTEMENTS are taken next. The student throws one leg high to front, side or back, the knee straight and the foot pointed, keeping the rest of the body as still and as upright as possible so that the hip joint is loosened. This vigorous exercise both warms and stretches the legs before the concise, tightening movements to come.

Aurora begins her solo in the Vision Scene of " The Sleeping Beauty " with a series of grands battements *rising on to the toe* (*p. 39, Figure 42*), *followed by* RACCOURCIS FERMÉS (*closing*) *as she comes down, repeated sixteen times on alternate legs, coming forward from the centre back stage.* (*N.B.* Since the time of writing, this solo has been altered by Ashton for the Royal Ballet. The steps described above are those of the Petipa choreography.)

If the student permits the body to sway in order to throw the leg higher, the hip joint is not considerably loosened and so the student negates the purpose for which the exercise is designed.

If either of these two important exercises are left until later in the class, the following exercises will tend to tighten the muscles, which will become over-developed and eventually bunch, hampering the dancer's movements.

BATTEMENTS TENDUS follow, in which one leg slides out along the floor until the foot is fully pointed (sometimes called DÉGAGÉ), and then steadily closes again.

Almost invariably before pirouetting outward, male dancers do a battement tendu *to the side before sinking into the preparatory position.*

Next comes BATTEMENTS DÉGAGÉS (or BATTEMENTS TENDUS or BATTEMENTS TENDUS JETÉS or BATTEMENTS TENDUS GLISSÉS or BATTEMENTS GLISSÉS) when the foot slides out just clear of the floor.

Battements tendus and *dégagés* should be quite even, beginning at a slow tempo and steadily quickening; both are designed to help the student to accustom himself to the feeling of fully stretching the leg, and to know exactly where the foot is on the floor: he will therefore know just when to spring in such movements as ASSEMBLÉ and will automatically stretch his legs. If the movements are performed jerking the foot out and in again, the dancer will find it more difficult to time such jumps, and so will waver in the air and land unsteadily.

BATTEMENTS RELEVÉS follow, in which the foot is first taken out as far as it will go on the floor (*tendu*), and the heel lowered and raised again (*relevé*) before closing. This is designed to strengthen the instep; some of the weight of the body must be taken on the working foot, for otherwise the instep will not become strong for *relevés* and little jumps, and the preparations for PIROUETTES, when one makes the same transference of weight between the legs, will be unsteady. (Also called *battements tendus relevés*).

There are three RONDS DE JAMBE, the first two of which are designed to increase the turn-out of the legs:

1. A TERRE, in which one foot describes a semi-circle on the floor, moving steadily with the toe on the ground from the front to side, side to back, and then past the stationary heel (PASSÉ) in a straight line to the front again. The movement can be performed in reverse. The accents are on the moment when the heels pass, and the moment when the foot is at the side; if the student is allowed to make the accents at the front and back, he may cross the pointed toe in front or behind the supporting foot, when it becomes difficult to avoid turning in the legs, so ruining the turn-out which is so important in the conquest of most ballet steps.

These are uncommon on the stage: however, the solo for " Winter " in Ashton's " Cinderella " commences with ronds de jambe à terre, and every time the initial theme returns in the orchestra the dancer performs the same step (p. 36, Figure 40).

When this movement is made with the supporting knee bent it becomes a GRAND *rond de jambe à terre* (see p. 54, Figure 62).

2. GRAND *rond de jambe* EN L'AIR, in which the dancer swings one leg round in the air from the front to the side and through to the back, or in the reverse direction (p. 54, Figure 59). If the leg only travels half way round the movement is called DEMI *grand rond de jambe en l'air*.

After Myrtha has commanded Giselle to dance with Albrecht, their pas de deux commences with Giselle performing a grand rond de jambe en l'air EN DEHORS *with the right leg, supported by Albrecht who then sways her from side to side.*

3. *Rond de jambe en l'air*, which is often performed together with RETIRÉS, as both make the knee flexible and make the student aware of the exact height of the raised foot: also it is important that *rond de jambe*, a very difficult movement, should first be practised with some support. The foot is raised to the side on a level with the other calf, the raised knee straight, and then describes an elongated oval between that point and the other calf, the leg from hip to knee remaining stationary (p. 54, Figure 60). Later this is

35

FIGURE 39   FIGURE 40

complicated by one or two tiny circles in the air (PETITS *ronds de jambe en l'air*) described by the foot close to the calf before it extends again (p. 54, Figure 63). The whole movement is then called DOUBLE *rond de jambe en l'air*.

If the leg is raised too high in this exercise the hips will sway about, destroying the balance so important in such a difficult movement: also the foot will be unable to come right in to the supporting leg in the *petit rond de jambe en l'air*, unless the dancer lowers his knee every time the foot comes in, which is even worse for the balance and makes the hips sway still more.

Odette's solo in Act 2 of " Swan Lake " begins with double ronds de jambe en l'air EN DEDANS *performed three times on alternate feet* (*Figure* 39).

The leading male dancer in Balanchine's " Theme and Variations " performs a series of double ronds de jambe en l'air EN DEHORS SAUTÉS *with the right leg while jumping off the left; he then steps forward on the right foot, raising the left behind him and closing it almost immediately to begin again. This whole sequence is performed eight times* (*p.* 39, *Figure* 41).

To perform RETIRÉS, the dancer draws one foot up as far as it will go while still touching the other leg, and then closes it down again. The main purpose of this exercise is to discover the student's " knee height ": this is an individual characteristic, and the raised foot does not necessarily touch the other knee, but the term means the height to which the foot can be raised while still touching the supporting leg. This contact is important, because once the raised leg is lifted any further and the foot begins to spring out from the supporting leg the dancer's hips must be considerably out of alignment, a fatal thing for a student's balance. Finished dancers will sometimes assume positions in which the hips are violently out of alignment, which they are able to do because of habits of balance formed during years of training. A dancer who is very tightly knit may not even get his foot as high as the supporting knee, whereas extremely loose ones may raise the foot well above it. When a PETIT *retiré* is performed the foot is raised only just off the ground; its purpose is to increase flexibility of the foot. *The dancer begins the third solo in the " Swan Lake " pas de trois with six* retirés *on alternative toes (Figure 44), which series recur three times more in her dance before she runs to the front corner of the stage.*

BATTEMENTS FRAPPÉS are designed to prepare the legs for jumping. The raised foot touches the other ankle, relaxed (p. 77, Figure 103) and from there the leg from the knee down is thrown out to the side with all possible force, without moving the knee (p. 77, Figure 108). After a short pause the foot is returned to the ankle.

Sometimes students lower the whole leg as the foot flies out so that the tip of the toe falls to the floor, which causes the knee to drop and rise again as the foot returns to the ankle. This turns a single movement into a double one and produces those odd stammering jumps occasionally seen to-day.

PETITS BATTEMENTS are designed to prepare the legs for beaten steps. The heel of one foot touches the other ankle (*sur le cou-de-pied*) while the underneath of the raised toes touches the floor, the knee bent. The lower part of the leg moves out and in, either changing from the front to the back of the supporting leg, or remaining on one or other, when it is called SERRÉ.
To conclude the pas de deux *in Act 2 of " Swan Lake," Siegfried walks round holding Odette's right hand above her head and her left hand at the side while she performs* petits battements sur le cou-de-pied serrés (p. 39, Figure 43).

If, instead of taking the foot out and in, the student merely waggles it backwards and forwards in a small semi-circle, he will weaken his knees, and also will fail to acquire the feeling of taking the leg out and in so essential to the cleanness of beats. He turns up his toes to relax the foot and thus avoid clenching it in his efforts to beat faster, which habit would be likely to return when he is attempting beaten steps, for which this exercise is designed, and so tighten up his legs that his whole body shakes with his exertions instead of allowing the legs to move freely.

In *battements* BATTUS the dancer moves the whole leg, without bending the knee or pointing the foot, to the side and closes alternately behind and in front.

To perform a DÉVELOPPÉ the dancer draws one foot up touching the other leg and extends it (*développé*). This movement should be practised slowly and evenly so that the student gains full control of the raised leg; this movement can also be performed while jumping (*développé* SAUTÉ). See also BALLOTTÉ.

Immediately before Odette falls into Benno's arms at the conclusion of the " Swan Lake " Act 2 pas de deux, she performs a développé *to the side with the left leg (see also previous example).*

The second half of the first male solo in the " Peasant " pas de deux from " Giselle " consists of développé sauté *to the side (Figure 45),* COUPÉ, ASSEMBLÉ *to the side twice repeated travelling from the audience's left to right, followed by two* ENTRECHATS SIX, SOUS-SUS *and* DOUBLE TOUR EN L'AIR. *The entire sequence is then repeated in the opposite direction to conclude the solo.*

(*N.B.* A *développé sauté* followed by a *coupé* and *assemblé* as described above are frequently described as SISSONE DOUBLÉE or SISSONE RETOMBÉE.)

Développé can also be performed PASSÉ, when the foot is passed from the front to the back (or the reverse), the knee bending as the extended foot passes the supporting leg. Examples will be found under ÉCHAPPÉ and SISSONE.

The dancer will usually finish *barre* by repeating a series of *grands battements* and *grands battements* EN CLOCHE which will loosen his hips again.

To perform *grands battements en cloche* the dancer throws his leg from a position high in front of him past the other leg to the back as high as he can while keeping the body upright, so that the hips are loosened as much as possible.

The second sailor's solo in " Fancy Free " begins with grands battements en cloche (*p.* 40, *Figure* 46).

If the body is not held upright the hips will not be loosened, and the student will find himself able to raise his leg less high off the floor from day to day.

BATTEMENTS BALANÇOIRES, or GRANDS BATTEMENTS JETÉS BALANCÉS, should not be confused with *battements en cloche*. In *battements balançoires* the leg swings backwards and forwards in the same way, but the dancer allows his body to sway forwards

FIGURE 41

FIGURE 42

FIGURE 43

FIGURE 44

FIGURE 46

FIGURE 45

FIGURE 47

and backwards in opposition to the leg, with one hand gliding to and fro along the *barre*. The purpose of this exercise is quite different: to prepare the dancer for the many steps he will perform in which the body is not vertical in the air. If he clings on to the *barre* while doing this, the purpose of the exercise is destroyed.

Sometimes before leaving the *barre* the dancers may perform loosening exercises (known as LIMBERING), which are many and various: for instance, the dancer puts one foot on the *barre* in front, to the side or behind him, and then slides in that direction with the knees straight into a kind of splits; or he may take one foot in his hand and pull it up with the knee straight in front or at the side, as close to his body as he can—which is called DÉTIRÉ or LE PIED DANS LA MAIN, or he may just stand and touch his toes, etc. Détiré *is seen on the stage during the first of the sailor's solos in "Fancy Free" when the sailor is standing on the bar (Figure 47).*

However, if the student studies in a method suitable to him (see p. 79) this should be unnecessary, as it often spoils the spring of an ARQUÉ dancer and will never alter the formation of his legs and allow him to become JARRETÉ: but for those *jarreté* dancers who desire to acquire even higher extensions than come naturally these exercises may be helpful.

The student now leaves the *barre* and comes into the centre of the classroom: having exercised his legs, he now performs a series of movements designed to exercise the upper part of his body, which are called PORTS DE BRAS although they include movements of the body (CAMBRÉ), shoulders (ÉPAULEMENT) and head as well as the arms. These parts of the body should all move harmoniously between one position of the arms and another, a co-ordination difficult to achieve considering the many possible combinations of the head and arms (see pp. 12–13; TEMPS LIÉ).

Next comes what is called CENTRE PRACTICE, PETIT ADAGIO or EXERCICES AU MILIEU, in which the *barre* exercises are elaborated without support. This is the dancer's final daily check on the state of his muscles and control, as after this point he co-ordinates his dancing instead of concentrating on separate movements.

Next comes the ADAGIO or GRAND ADAGIO section of class, which has three main purposes: (1) to help the student so to control and co-ordinate all his movements that they gain a steady flow; (2) to improve his balance—an important part of which is developing the knack of " throwing his weight "; (3) to make him so aware of his positions that they become second nature.

(1) In almost all these exercises the movements are slow and even; for instance, throughout sixteen bars of music the student may slowly complete one long unfolding movement; say, by drawing one foot up to the other knee, extending it in front, then as he steadily turns taking the raised foot right round to the back and drawing it into the knee again, as he ends the turn facing the front. (2) Balance can mean anything from simply rising on to the toe of one foot to the complicated series of movements which make up a PIROUETTE RENVERSÉ EN DEDANS, and also includes the transference of weight from one leg on to the other extended leg:

for instance, the dancer may step forward three or four feet on to his toes, and as he does so take the body over the front leg while raising the other leg behind him. This knack of " throwing the weight " steadily is one of the hardest things to develop, and one of the easiest to lose. (3) With plenty of time to spare, the student can take care of the positions through which his body passes and those with which he concludes a phrase of movement, and can consider their many angles in relation to the audience (see DIRECTIONS; ÉPAULEMENT).

With practice the movements in *adagio* become more complicated; so immediately on stepping forward (as described in (2) above) he would be required simultaneously to turn on the supporting leg while the body inclines at an oblique angle; or he might stand in a pose with one leg extended behind and slowly incline the body forward (PENCHÉ) as the leg rises behind him.

Next follows ALLEGRO which consists mainly of jumping steps and therefore does not allow the student time to consider any of the problems set out above, which will now solve themselves either automatically or not at all, for there is no time to think. Even after the dancer's positions, control and balance in fast-moving steps are perfect he is still faced with the problem of giving each step its particular character, which is the hall-mark of the artist.

Towards the end of class, while the girls put on their blocked point shoes, the boys practise the feats generally allotted to them, such as DOUBLE TOURS EN L'AIR, COUPÉS JETÉS EN TOURNANT, SAUTÉS PIROUETTES, etc. Finally the girls practise in their point shoes, at first steps on both feet to accustom themselves to the feeling of the shoes, and later steps on one foot, working up to *pirouettes en diagonale* and FOUETTÉ ROND DE JAMBE EN TOURNANT.

Throughout class the teacher may invent exercises as he goes along, or rely on set exercises; or both, in which case the student will not be slow at tackling new problems, which he is constantly called upon to do in the rehearsal room; whereas the set exercises will instil in him the habit of continuing to perfect movements with which he is extremely familiar, sometimes to the point of boredom —which may apply to many of the roles he will perform hundreds of times during his career.

When class is over, it is not uncommon for dancers to practise the DOUBLE WORK they will perform together in the evening; because, exactly as is the case with all the movements described above, one loses the feeling of this after a few days without practice—which is why dancers hate Mondays.

CLASSICAL

1. CLASSICAL BALLET (not to be confused with BALLET D'ÉCOLE).
Classical is a word which has been used in so many ways in the
ballet world that it can now mean almost anything. One of the
reasons for the complication of thought here is the fact that once a
ballet has been performed for several generations it becomes " a
classic," and for this reason ballets are often called classical although
they may be nothing of the sort.

In fact the words classical, romantic and narrative when used in
their correct sense could be equally useful in the discussion of
ballet as in the discussion of painting: a classical ballet would be one
in which the form, pattern and movement are the primary considera-
tion: a romantic ballet one in which the conveyance of a mood is the
raison d'être of the work: and "narrative ballet" would be used to describe those the purpose of which was the relation of a series of events.

The ballets of Imperial Russia surviving to-day contain long
and complicated stories, but these serve merely as a peg on which
to hang the dancing; therefore as the dances are the focal point
these ballets are not narrative but classical in intention. Similarly,
although " Le Spectre de la Rose " is based on a poem by
Gautier, as in the poem it is the creation of mood which counts
in the ballet, for which the story provides an excuse, and the ballet
is therefore romantic. " Giselle "—which is sometimes lumped in
with " classical ballets " because it is " a classic," and at other
times called a romantic ballet because it arose as a product of the
Romantic movement of the early 19th century—is in fact a narrative ballet, because the story is most important, as will be recognised
by those who have seen it performed as a dramatic ballet.

The Bolshoi, excelling as they do in romantic and narrative
ballet, made a superlatively good job of " Giselle ", as did Ballet
Rambert; when this work is performed, however, by a company
less excellent in this type of ballet, such as the Royal Ballet, even
the performance of such a fine romantic performer as Beriosova in
the leading role cannot induce a parallel romanticism in the *corps
de ballet* who remain cold and disinterested; the same is true of the
Royal Ballet's production of " Les Sylphides ". Strangely enough
the performance of the Kirov in the latter ballet, though this
company is predominantly " classical ", was the finest to be seen
since the choreographer's death—presumably because the company
have put themselves out, since Fokine made this work for them
over 60 years ago, to preserve the spirit as well as the exact choreography of the ballet.

2. CLASSICAL DANCER. Dancers who appear in the leading roles in old ballets are often considered " classical dancers," and from this generalisation it is erroneously presumed that they are suited to all those various roles.

Dancers could be classified in the same manner as that in which ballets are classified above: the classical dancers being those whose primary appeal is to the eye of the spectator, because they are concerned with presenting all the niceties of movement in the choreography: whereas the romantic dancers appeal primarily to the emotions, being concerned with using the theme and movements to express a mood: while the narrative dancer appeals primarily to the intellect of the spectator because he or she concentrates on ensuring that every situation is clearly conveyed to the audience. These categories could apply to any theatrical performer.

It will be seen therefore that if dancers were only cast in roles which, owing to their physique (see ARQUÉ), came naturally to them—instead of spending much energy trying to get away with something physically awkward to them, as is common to-day—one would then be able to appreciate or enjoy the individual way in which each dancer would attack a role, and prefer the classical approach, the romantic or the narrative according to taste.

3. CLASSICAL THEATRICAL DANCING. Term used by Blasis, Cecchetti and others as synonymous with " ballet dancing ", which could well bear revival to-day, when so many choreographers lean to the classical while ignoring the theatrical: in fact the latter adjective has become virtually a term of abuse in ballet criticism.

CLASSICISM

When it is said of a dancer that she shows classicism, this usually means that she performs steps as taught in ballet class without affectation or mannerism.

CLOCHE, EN. See CLASS, *battements* (p. 38)

CLOSED POSITION. See FERMÉ; FEET, POSITIONS OF THE

CODA. See ADAGE

COLLÉ. See also SOUBRESAUT

In jumping steps performed *collé* the legs and feet do not beat, but cling tightly together in the air. It is an essential part of some steps; others can be performed *collé*, when the continuity of the movement is momentarily broken as the feet cling together.

COMPOUND STEP

1. A step made up of two or more others so combined as to create one movement distinctly their own, i.e. COUPÉ JETÉ EN TOURNANT, BRISÉ VOLÉ or CONTRETEMPS. 2. A sequence of steps frequently combined, i.e. TOUR DE REINS (see JETÉ, p. 72).

CONTRETEMPS

The dancer stands with the left foot behind him.

1. As the right heel rises, the dancer describes a little circle just clear of the floor with the left foot, bringing it round to the front and replacing the right, which then slides out to the side with the body leaning over it. Both knees bend, and the dancer jumps up with the left leg raised behind (Figure 49) while continuing to travel in the same direction. Landing on the right foot, he slides the left in front, when he is ready to repeat the *contretemps* to the other side.

2. Occasionally one sees the full and more difficult *contretemps* in which the dancer closes the left leg behind the right as both knees bend before springing out.

The male dancer makes his entrance in the " Blue Bird" pas de deux performing a contretemps (*p. 47, Figure 49*), *followed by an* assemblé porté battu (*p. 14, Figure 22*).

DEMI-CONTRETEMPS. The spring off the right foot and sliding forward movement of the left with which the dancer concludes a *contretemps* (*temps levé en arabesque, chassé passé*).

CORPS DE BALLET

In pre-Diaghileff days, the *corps de ballet* held an individual status and no member thereof performed anything other than *corps de ballet* dances—that is to say dances performed by an even number of dancers, usually all doing the same step at the same moment in perfect symmetry. Their purpose was solely to support and frame the soloists and the ballerina. To-day, however, the line of demarcation between one rank and another is no longer rigid: the term *corps de ballet* is used relative to a particular ballet under discussion, not in qualifying a dancer, for nearly all dancers save the most exalted appear from time to time as members of the *corps de ballet*. It was Massine with his " symphonic " experiments who demonstrated that it is no longer necessary in classical ballets for a *corps de ballet* to move in exactly symmetrical formations, and choreographers such as Tudor, van Dantzig, Tetley and Morrice have eliminated the conventional *corps* and created ballets in which each character has individuality.

(*N.B.* The term *corps de ballet* can also be used to mean the entire company.)

CORYPHÉE. See also BALLERINA

A rank existing in the Imperial Russian Ballet given to those dancers not principals, but performing in small groups as distinct from the large mass of the *corps de ballet* and classified between that group and the soloists. This rank is correctly a specific one; but the designation is incorrectly used today by some English companies to signify " small soloist ".

CÔTÉ, DE. See ATTITUDE; DIRECTIONS

COU DE PIED. See LEG, POSITIONS OF THE, and CLASS (p. 37) ; *TEMPS DE*, see SOUS-SUS

COUPÉ. See also JETÉ (*coupé*) (p. 72)

A joining step used to transfer the weight of the body: basically, it is no more than to put down one foot while picking up the other.

The dancer brings the left foot (which may be extended or close to the other) in to replace the right, which rises slightly to touch the left ankle. A *coupé* can be performed with the knees either bent or straight, or with a little jump, when a beat may be added.

A *coupé* EN TOURNANT is in fact a turn on the right foot while replacing it by the left.

(*N.B.* When in *coupé* the weight is taken from the back foot to the front foot, the *coupé* is said to be DESSUS (over). When the weight is taken from the front foot to the back, the *coupé* is said to to DESSOUS (under).)

COUPÉ DE CARACTÈRE

The dancer begins almost in fifth position, but the left knee is slightly bent and the left heel raised a little from the floor. He then transfers his weight on to the toes of the left foot and stretches the left knee so that the right foot comes slightly off the ground. The right foot is not pointed. *Coupés de caractère* are usually performed in a series in which the dancer immediately returns his weight to the right foot, which movement is accented, giving the sequence a lilting effect, which is particularly effective when performed turning.

Coupé de caractère performed in a series is the basis of most of the movements of the Polovtsian Women in Fokine's " Dances from Prince Igor " (Figure 48), and can also frequently be observed in the Dance of the Princesses in the same choreographer's " Firebird."

COURONNE, EN. See p. 13, Figure 19

FIGURE 48   FIGURE 49

COURSE, PAS DE

A smooth succession of running steps performed forwards and with the minimum of turn-out. This is one of the most difficult movements to accomplish smoothly and with ease on the stage. Evdokimova, Fukagawa, Michael Ho, Samsova and Nureyev are particularly notable for their striking *pas de course*.

COURU, PAS. See BOURRÉE, PAS DE; PAS COURU

CROISÉ. See DIRECTIONS; FEET, POSITIONS OF THE; p. 53, Figures 50, 55; p. 13, Figures 15, 18, 20

CROIX, EN

In class, a series of BATTEMENTS or DÉVELOPPÉS done moving one leg to the front, side, back, side or to the back, side, front, side, thus marking out three lines of a cross. BALLONNÉS, ASSEMBLÉS, etc. can also be done *en croix*.

CUISSE, TEMPS DE or PAS DE

The *sissonne's* stammering brother, consisting of a BATTEMENT DÉGAGÉ followed by a SISSONNE either SAUTÉ or SUR LES POINTES. The dancer extends the left foot to the side and then closes it as both knees bend, ready to spring sideways from the left leg which lingers behind and closes just after the right.

The feet never change in the *sissone*, as it is important that the body should lean the same way in the *sissonne* as at the moment when the knees bend. Consequently, depending on the preparatory *battement dégagé*, *temps de cuisse* are DESSOUS, DESSUS, DEVANT or DERRIÉRE. They can also be performed EN AVANT and EN ARRIÈRE, and with a RETIRÉ instead of the *dégagé*.

DANCE DIRECTOR

The choreographer of present-day musicals or films.

DANCE NOTATION. See NOTATION

DANCING, SEVEN MOVEMENTS IN. See MOVEMENTS, 7 CATEGORIES OF

DANSE COMIQUE. See also CHARACTER DANCE

Folk Dance, the dance of the people. In the 18th and early 19th centuries what we now call character dancing was termed *danse comique*.

DANSE DE CIRCULATION or DANSE DE PARCOURS

A style of dancing covering a large portion of the stage. This style is only to be observed in the performance of dancers accustomed to perform on really large stages, for instance the Scala, Milan, or the Bolshoi, Moscow, 125 and 85 feet wide respectively.

DANSEUR. DANSEUSE. See also OPERATIC DANCER

A male dancer. A female dancer.

DANSEUR CLOS or BOWLEGGED. See ARQUÉ

DANSEUR NOBLE or DANSEUR SERIEUX

A term seldom used to-day. At one time all dancers and dances were divided into three categories: *noble*, *demi-caractère* and *caractère*, this being in the days when everyone was considered to be exclusively possessed of one of seven characters or " humours," as in the plays of Jonson and his period. Ballet, in keeping with this current idea, fixed the characters of dancers upon their visual aspect, and consequently *danseurs nobles*, who were always the heroes—rather like tenors in opera—were always tall and danced stately dances. If on the other hand the dancer was short it was presumed that he was energetic and uncouth, and he was given either the villainous, comical or peasant role. Needless to say this belief is no longer held, and consequently such arbitrary classifications are much more rare; one recognises the hero by his actions, not by his physical appearance.

When the term *danseur noble* is used to-day it generally implies a tall dancer of fine appearance and good manners towards his partner; Dowell is an obvious example.

DÉBOITÉ. See EMBOITÉ

DÉBOULÉS. See TOURS, DEMI-

DÉCOR

Theatrical decoration. Originally this term covered scenery, properties and costumes; to-day it can mean scenery and properties alone.

DEDANS, EN. See pp. 54–55

DÉFILÈ, LE GRAND

A spectacular walking parade often in use in Continental opera houses on opening or closing nights of seasons during which the stage is slowly filled with all the members of the ballet company, commencing with the most junior members and progressing in strict order of precedence to the stars.

DÉGAGÉ. See LEG, POSITIONS OF THE; CLASS, *battements tendus* and *battements dégagés* (*p.* 34)

DÉGAGÉ, GRAND. See POSÉ; FOUETTÉ GRAND

DEGREES, 45°, 90°. See LEG, POSITIONS OF THE (p. 77)

DEHORS, EN. See p. 54 ; *L'EN DEHORS*
See TURN-OUT

DEMI. See p. 77, Figures 105, 109 ; FOOT, POSITIONS OF
THE ; ACHILLES TENDON

DERRIÈRE. See p. 52

DESCENDANT, EN. See DIRECTIONS

DESSUS. DESSOUS. See p. 52

DÉTIRÉ. See CLASS, Limbering (p. 41)

DÉTOURNÉ. See also ASSEMBLÉ SUR LES POINTES ;
BASQUE, PAS DE

DEMI-*détourné*.—The dancer stands with one foot in front of the
other, either together or apart, rises on the toes and swivels round
to face the opposite direction.
Détourné.—This is performed with the feet close together.
(*a*) The dancer crosses the left leg round in front of the right,
slightly bending the left knee so that the left foot is behind the
right. (*b*) He then rises on both toes and swivels round to face
the front again. The right foot is once more in front.
This movement may also be performed EN DEHORS when the
dancer crosses the right foot behind the left before turning.

DEUX, PAS DE. See also PAS; DOUBLE WORK; ADAGE
A dance performed by two people.

DEVANT. See ATTITUDE and p. 52

DÉVELOPPÉ or *BATTEMENT DÉVELOPPÉ.*
See CLASS (p. 38); BALLOTTÉ; ÉTENDU; FLÈCHE, TEMPS
DE; SISSONE

DIAGONALE, EN. See DIRECTIONS

DIRECTIONS or *SENS*
1. The movement of the dancer travelling over the stage.
2. The position of the dancer's body in relation to the audience.
3. The position of the legs in relation to the rest of the body.
Though the terms which indicate to the dancer in what relation
to the audience—either on the spot or travelling—he is to place

himself are confusing, this affects dancers less than one would expect because ballet is taught by example, not by the book; therefore a choreographer may be surrounded by five dancers each knowing one step by a different name, or no name at all, without detrimental effect on the ballet.

Cecchetti numbered the points of the room in the attempt to clarify matters; unfortunately this idea has since been used by other teachers using different numbering.

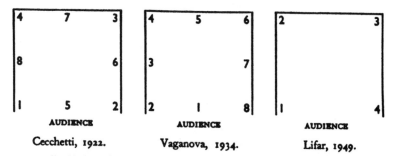

Cecchetti, 1922.   Vaganova, 1934.   Lifar, 1949.

1. The movement of the dancer travelling over the stage.

EN DESCENDANT.—The dancer travels from the back to the front of the stage.

EN RECULANT.—The reverse of *en descendant*.

EN DIAGONALE.—The dancer travels diagonally across the stage.

DE CÔTÉ.—The dancer travels from one side of the stage to the other. (*N.B.* The dancer need not face *de côté* when he is travelling *de côté*, see below.)

2. The position of the dancer's body in relation to the audience.

Positions are said to be either DE FACE (facing the audience); CROISÉ, ÉFFACÉ or ÉCARTÉ (facing a corner); DE CÔTÉ (facing the wings). In any position performed with the dancer's back to the audience the words EN FACE (or DOS AU PUBLIC) may be added.

DE FACE.—The dancer's body faces the audience squarely, also called EN FACE.

CROISÉ.—Facing a corner or the wings, the dancer stands with his front leg nearest the audience, his back leg furthest away.

ÉFFACÉ.—Facing a corner or the wings, the dancer stands with his front leg furthest from the audience, his back leg nearest.

ÉCARTÉ.—The dancer stands with his whole body facing a corner, his feet to either side, with one raised or both on the ground.

Croisé and *éffacé* are used unqualified, when the dancer is facing a corner, the fact that he is placed diagonally to the audience then being implicit: whereas when he faces the wings DE CÔTÉ is added.

(*N.B. Croisé* is also used to describe one of the fourth POSITIONS OF THE FEET. Unfortunately it is also sometimes used to define ÉPAULEMENTS and in place of OPPOSITION as the converse of an OUVERTE POSITION OF THE ARMS, which latter creates the anomaly of a position *éffacé* with *croisé* arms.

In some systems, OUVERTE is used instead of *éffacé* as a position of the legs opposite to *croisé*, and also as a position of the arms the converse of opposition, creating still further confusion.)

DIRECTIONS OF THE BODY, EIGHT

Eight poses designed by Cecchetti to make the student aware of the relation of his body to the audience. See Figures 50 to 57.

3. The position of the legs in relation to the rest of the body.

EN AVANT.—Forwards; EN ARRIÈRE.—Backwards. (ASSEMBLÉS *en avant* and *en arrière* do not travel unless PORTÉ is added.)

DEVANT.—In front; DERRIÈRE.—Behind.

Devant. Indicates that (1) one leg is extended in front of the dancer; or (2) in ASSEMBLÉS, BALLONNÉS, GLISSADES, JETÉS À LA SECONDE and DE CÔTÉ, RETIRÉS, SISSONNES and TEMPS DE CUISSE, the leg extended to the side opens from and closes in front of the other ; or (3) in PAS DE BOURRÉE *devant*—also a sideways movement—the leg first extended must close both times in front of the other, its original position being immaterial.

Derrière. Indicates that (1) one leg is extended behind the dancer; or (2) in ASSEMBLÉS, BALLONNÉS, GLISSADES, JETÉS À LA SECONDE and DE CÔTÉ, RETIRÉS, SISSONNES and TEMPS DE CUISSE, the leg extended to the side opens from and closes behind the other ; or (3) in PAS DE BOURRÉE *derrière*—also a sideways movement—the leg first extended must close both times behind the other, its original position being immaterial.

DESSUS.—Over ; DESSOUS.—Under (see also COUPÉ).

Dessus. Indicates that (1) in ASSEMBLÉS, BALLONNÉS, GLISSADES, JETÉS À LA SECONDE and DE CÔTÉ, RETIRÉS, SISSONNES and TEMPS DE CUISSE, the leg extended to the side begins behind the other and closes in front of it ; (2) in PAS DE BOURRÉE the leg first extended must close (*a*) in front of and (*b*) behind the other, its original position being immaterial.

Dessous. Indicates that (1) in ASSEMBLÉS, BALLONNÉS, GLISSADES, JETÉS À LA SECONDE and DE CÔTÉ, RETIRÉS, SISSONNES and TEMPS DE CUISSE, the leg extended to the side begins in front of the other and closes behind it ; (2) in PAS DE BOURRÉE the leg first extended must close (*a*) behind and (*b*) in front of the other, its original position being immaterial.

FIGURE 50.
CROISÉ DEVANT.

FIGURE 51.
QUATRIÈMÉ DEVANT.

FIGURE 52.
ÉCARTÉ.

FIGURE 53.
SECONDE.

FIGURE 54.
ÉPAULÉ.

FIGURE 55.
CROISÉ DERRIÈRE.

FIGURE 56.
QUATRIÈME DERRIÈRE.

FIGURE 57.
ÉFFACÉ.

FIGURE 58.
PIROUETTE DEDANS SUR
LA POINTE.

FIGURE 59.
GRAND ROND DE JAMBE
EN L'AIR EN DEDANS

FIGURE 60.
ROND DE JAMBE EN L'AIR
EN DEDANS.

EN DEHORS—Outwards: EN DEDANS—Inwards (see also FOUETTÉ)
En dehors. Indicates that in (1) turns, the dancer's body turns
backwards ; in other words, when the dancer stands on his right
leg and turns anti-clockwise, the movement is *en dehors* and the
same applies when he stands on his left leg and turns clockwise.
(2) RONDS DE JAMBE À TERRE, and GRAND *rond de jambe* EN L'AIR,
the leg moves backward from the front or side. (3) *Rond de
jambe en l'air* the raised foot describes an oval in
the following sequence : side, front, back, side.

FIGURE 61.
SAUTÉ PIROUETTE EN
DEHORS À LA SECONDE.

FIGURE 62.
GRAND ROND DE JAMBE
A TERRE EN DEHORS

FIGURE 63.
PETIT ROND DE JAMBE EN
L'AIR EN DEDANS.

En dedans. Indicates that in (1) turns, the dancer's body faces the
direction in which he is turning ; in other words, when the
dancer stands on his left leg and turns anti-clockwise, the move-

ment is *en dedans* and the same applies when he stands on his right leg and turns clockwise. (2) RONDS DE JAMBE A TERRE, and GRAND *rond de jambe* EN L'AIR, the leg moves forward from the back or side. (3) *Rond de jambe en l'air* the raised foot describes an elongated oval in the following sequence : side, back, front, side.

DIVERTISSEMENT

Formerly a suite of dances inserted as a series of show pieces into a ballet, bearing little or no relation to the story but designed to exploit the talents of dancers not otherwise concerned in the plot. A major example of this may be found in the last act of " The Sleeping Beauty," in the dances of the fairy-tale characters, included under the slight pretext that they are doing honour to Princess Aurora; a minor example in the first act of " Giselle," where the " Peasant " *pas de deux* was inserted some time after the première of the ballet, simply to display the talents of two principal dancers whose absence from the performance might have disappointed their audience.

To-day the term " *divertissement* " is applied to any ballet containing no story, theme or mood, in which the sole aim of the choreographer is to display his dancers to the best advantage. In this aim is demonstrated the essential difference between a *divertissement* and an abstract ballet, for in the latter individual characteristics are, or should be, subjugated to the visual patterns designed by the choreographer to parallel and/or complement his aural impressions of the music.

DOUBLE WORK or PAS DE DEUX or PARTNER-ING. See also ADAGE ; ENLÉVEMENT ; PIROUETTE ; PORTEUR ; PROMENADE ; POISSON, PAS ; PORTÉ

All movements when one dancer is partnered by another, and also movements when, for example, two or three male dancers lift one girl. Because it is a comparatively recent development in ballet, there are very few terms exclusively used to describe double work. Soviet dancers and choreographers have made a special feature of double work and developed it to a degree quite unparalleled in the West, partly because their circumstances enable them to begin practising together at an early age. Complicated lifts and throws are a means of adding excitement and exhilaration to spectacular " concert numbers " but are also used with poetry and subtlety in their long ballets. Gradually some of the daring developments of Soviet *pas de deux* are being included in the work of Western choreographers ; for examples see pages 60–61.

DOS AU PUBLIC. See DIRECTIONS

ÉCART, LE GRAND

The splits: hence the name sometimes substituted for PAS CISEAUX or *écart* EN L'AIR, since the dancer springs up into this position.

ÉCARTÉ. See DIRECTIONS (pp. 51, 53)

ÉCHAPPÉ or *TEMPS ÉCHAPPÉ*

Both feet spring out simultaneously sideways, or to front and back.

The dancer may (1) spring out on to the toes, in which position the knees do not bend; (2) spring out landing on the flat foot with both knees bent. When the latter is performed with a big jump beats may be added (sometimes called ROYALE or ENTRECHAT OUVERT); with a very slight jump, the movement outward is often a preparation for PIROUETTES (échappé ELANCÉ).

Shortly after the opening of the female dancer's variation in the " Blue Bird" pas de deux, when she first comes down to the front right-hand corner of the stage, she performs two échappés *on tiptoe, followed by a* DÉVELOPPÉ PASSÉ EN ARRIÈRE *while performing three hops on her left toe, and a* PAS DE BOURRÉE *on the spot: the whole sequence is repeated twice more, travelling diagonally backwards (Figure 67).*

Franz begins his solo in Act 3 of " Coppélia " with échappés SAUTÉS battus *(Figure 64),* FERMÉ SAUTÉ battu *twice.*

FIGURE 64

ÉCOLE or *SCHOOL*.   See BALLET D'ÉCOLE; METHOD

ÉFFACÉ.   See DIRECTIONS (pp. 51, 53)

ÉLANCÉ.   See also MOVEMENTS IN DANCING; ÉCHAPPÉ

A jump performed *élancé* is done skimming along the floor, without a big spring. (Not to be confused with PORTÉ.)

ÉLÉVATION.   See also ACHILLES TENDON; PLANÉ

The dancer's ability to jump in the air, " steps of elevation " being the bigger jumps. (Not to be confused with BALLON.)

The height of elevation possessed by the dancer depends on the degree to which his legs are bowed plus the depth of his *demi-plié*. Nobody looking at a photograph of Nijinsky—famed for his fantastic elevation—can fail to notice his unmistakable bow legs : while it is said of him by his colleagues that he kept his heels on the ground while doing a full *plié* in fifth position.

Lifar states that elevation is the province of men alone, since great jumps " contrast too sharply with the delicate and fragile charm " of the ballerina. Anyone who has seen the Canadian, the Cuban, the Danish or the Soviet ballerinas dance will find it difficult to agree with him.

ÉLÈVE.   See BALLERINA.   *ÉLEVÉ*.   See RELEVÉ

EMBOITÉ.   See also JETÉ, PASSÉ (p. 75)

Usually seen in a series, when they resemble the movement of plaiting. The dancer stands on her toes with her legs together, then swings her back leg a little to the side and closes in front of

FIGURE 65

the other. If the foot is taken from the front and closed behind the step is DÉBOITÉ.

Both the Sugar Plum Fairy and the Prelude dancer in " Les Sylphides" perform emboîtés at the end of their solos.

The first steps of the eight attendants on the Lilac Fairy in the coda of the Prologue to " The Sleeping Beauty" are sixteen emboîtés coming forward (p. 57, Figure 65).

EN L'AIR. See AIR, EN L'

ENCHAÎNEMENT

A phrase, or pattern, of steps put together either for use on the stage, or for practice in class.

ENLÈVEMENT or LIFT. See also PORTÉ ; DOUBLE WORK

A dancer is lifted in the air in a step or pose (see pages 60 and 61).

ENTRECHAT. See also ÉCHAPPÉ; SISSONNE; ASSEMBLÉ

The dancer jumps straight up beating and changing the legs beneath him. If he lands on both feet the *entrechat* is even-numbered: if with one foot touching the supporting leg, the *entrechat* has an odd number.

In *entrechat* DEUX and TROIS, SIX and SEPT, DIX and ONZE, on landing the feet end having reversed their relationship ; whereas in QUATRE and CINQ, HUIT and NEUF, the feet return to their original relationship.

Entrechat DEUX (also called ROYALE or CHANGEMENT BATTU). The dancer springs, beats, changes his legs and lands on both feet. *Entrechat* TROIS: the same landing on one foot.

Entrechat QUATRE. The dancer springs, changes the legs, beats, changes the legs back to land in their original position. *Entrechat* CINQ: the same landing on one foot.

Entrechat SIX. The dancer springs, changes the legs, beats, changes them back, beats again before changing to land with the feet reversed. *Entrechat* SEPT: the same landing on one foot.

(*N.B.* In a GRAND *royale* or *entrechat six* SANS CHANGER the legs first beat, then change and beat, and change again to land with the feet in their original position.)

Entrechat HUIT. The dancer springs, changes the legs, beats, changes again and beats, changes a third time and beats before the legs change to land in their original position. *Entrechat* NEUF: the same landing on one foot.

FIGURE 66   FIGURE 67

The male dancer finishes his solo in the " Blue Bird" pas de deux
with six entrechats (*Figure 66*), *and a* DOUBLE TOUR EN L'AIR.

ENTRÉE. See also ADAGE   An entrance or opening dance.

ENTRELACÉE See JETÉ, p. 75

ENVELOPPÉ.   See also FLÈCHE, TEMPS DE; JETÉ
    ENVELOPPÉ

A movement used to give momentum to inward turns. The foot
extended behind the dancer swings round in the air to the side and
then round to the front of the other leg. The impetus thus gained
helps the dancer to turn, either on the ground or in the air.
Towards the end of the pas de deux *in " The Sleeping Beauty,"*
Act 3, Aurora runs diagonally down stage, supports herself by means
of the Prince's raised left arm with her left leg raised behind her,
performs an enveloppé, *turns and falls into a* FISH DIVE (*p. 93,*
Figure 118). *This sequence is performed three times.*

ÉPAULÉ. See DIRECTIONS (p. 53, Figure 54)

FIGURE 68

FIGURE 69

ENLÈVEMENT or LIFT

Figure 68 illustrates the entrance and exit of the two dancers in Messerer's " Melodie " ; while at the end of his " Spring Waters " the ballerina performs a *saut de basque* on to her partner's hand as he lifts her (Figure 69), then a *grand rond de jambe en l'air dehors*

FIGURE 70

FIGURE 71

with the right leg as he runs off the stage supporting her in the position illustrated in Figure 68; and Figure 71 shows yet another "stulchik" ("little chair") used by Ashton in "La Fille mal Gardée." Figure 70 shows one of the more spectacular throws in the "Moskowski Waltz" (Vainonen).

ÉPAULEMENT. See also DIRECTIONS (p. 52)

Literally " shouldering."

Initially, ballet students take all poses with the hips and shoulders square, which gives the pose a simple, honest appearance. This is later varied by turning the body from the waist upwards so that one shoulder is tilted forward and the other back, which is called *épaulement* and gives poses and movements an entirely different appearance.

As the student turns into profile, the pose—if the leg is raised to the front or the back—automatically becomes more clearly seen: to sharpen it still further by *épaulement* is striking but when this is invariably done students' poses become mannered and monotonous, for instead of each position having three possible directions of the trunk one angle alone is used.

ÉQUILIBRE or *APLOMB*

1. Balance. With practice this becomes very highly developed, as may be gathered from the fact that girls maintain their balance in mid-air throughout complicated lifts, men while performing *tours en l'air* or *coupés jetés.*

2. *Equilibre* also means to hold a pose on one toe. *While in* ATTITUDE (*Figure 72*) *Aurora balances* (équilibre) *while changing partners during the Rose Adagio in Act* 1 *of "The Sleeping Beauty".*

FIGURE 72

ÉTENDRE. See MOVEMENTS IN DANCING, 7

ÉTENDU or *ÉTENDRE LE GENOU*

A dancer standing on one or both legs in *plié* stretches his knee or knees. The term is also used when a dancer stretches his foot out from a position touching the other leg (also called *développé*).

ÉTOILE. See also BALLERINA, PRIMA

Star. The leading dancers of the Paris Opéra Ballet are known as *Première Danseuse Étoile* or *Premier Danseur Étoile.*

EXERCICES À LA BARRE; EXERCICES AU MILIEU. See CLASS (pp. 33 and 41 respectively)

EXTENDED. See LEG, POSITIONS OF THE; p. 13; HANDS, POSITIONS OF THE

EXTENSION. See LEG, POSITIONS OF THE

FACE, DE; FACE, EN. See DIRECTIONS

FAILLI or SISSONE CHASSÉ PASSÉ. See also PIGEON, TEMPS DE

The dancer springs into the air, landing on the front foot with the back foot raised (*sissone*), and then slides the back foot through to the front (CHASSÉ PASSÉ). This can be performed in reverse with the front foot moving through to the back (EN ARRIÈRE).

If the raised leg is merely tucked up on the front or back of the ankle before sliding through, the step is usually known as *sissone* SIMPLE *passé*, whereas if the leg is raised behind in attitude or arabesque (*sissone* EN AVANT), the term used is often *failli.* Sometimes *failli* is used only when a beat is added to the *sissone.*

(*N.B.* Failli is sometimes confused with DEMI-CONTRETEMPS.)

FAUX ENTRECHAT CINQ. See SISSONE

FEET, POSITIONS OF THE. See also FOOT, POSITIONS OF THE; TURN-OUT; ARABESQUE

Unlike most other terms in ballet, the five positions of the feet (p. 64) are standard to every method of teaching, and have been so since Beauchamp named them at the end of the 17th century; they are based on the principle of the turn-out of the legs first defined in Arbeau's *Orchésographie*, published 1588.

POSITIONS FERMÉES are the 1st, 3rd, 5th and Lifar's 6th, because the feet touch: POSITIONS OUVERTES are the 2nd, 4th and Lifar's 7th because the feet are apart.

If the dancer is standing in 2nd or 4th position and raises either foot, the leg straight and the weight of the body resting on the other leg, he is still standing in 2nd or 4th position but the words

POINTE TENDUE, DÉGAGÉ, DEMI, EN L'AIR, À LA HAUTEUR, or EXTENDED are added to indicate to which height the foot is raised.

FIGURE 73.
FIRST.

FIGURE 74.
SECOND.

FIGURE 75.
THIRD.

FIGURE 76.
FOURTH OUVERTE.

FIGURE 77.
FOURTH CROISÉ.

FIGURE 78.
FIFTH or THIRD.

FIGURE 79.
FIFTH CROISÉ or FIFTH.

FIGURE 80.
SIXTH (Lifar).

FIGURE 81.
SEVENTH (Lifar).

FERMÉ. See also FEET, POSITIONS OF THE

Closed. The dancer (1) closes one foot to the other: (2) closes both feet together: usually in fifth position.

When (1) is performed jumping, the terms used are *fermé sauté, assemblé serré, assemblé fermé, assemblé simple, assemblé coupé,* or *petit assemblé.* When (2) is performed with a beat the term used can be *royale fermé.*

FIGURANT, FIGURANTE or MARCHEUSE

"A ballet-dancer" is the definition given in the 12-vol. Oxford English Dictionary (1961). The translation of the word in Spiers French-English dictionary (1849) is given as: (1) figurant (dancer); (2) supernumerary. This synonymity of ballet dancer with " extra person engaged for odd jobs" (Oxford English) reflects the disrespect accorded to the ballet dancer in the 19th century.

FISH DIVE. See POISSON, PAS

FLÈCHE, TEMPS DE or ENVELOPPÉ DÉVELOPPÉ. See also GARGOUILLADE; PASSÉ

The dancer throws the right leg in front and springs, quickly withdrawing the right foot beneath him with that knee bent as the left foot is drawn up simultaneously behind it, passed through the gap over the right foot and quickly extended in front as he lands on the right leg. *Temps de flèche* is frequently performed by Soviet dancers turning once or twice in the air, when it resembles *jeté enveloppé.*

The Jester performs temps de flèche *in Ashton's " Cinderella."*

During the Danse des Mirlitons *in Act 2 of Ivanoff's "Casse-Noisette," when the leading dancer stands in the centre and the other four girls jump in towards her from the four corners of the stage performing* ASSEMBLÉS *she performs* temps de flèche, *two* PETITS JETÉS, *and four* RETIRÉS. *This sequence is four times repeated.*

FLIC-FLAC. See FOUETTÉ

FLOOR PATTERN. See PATTERN

FONDU. See also SOUTENU

1. A movement is finished with a soft slowing-down effect. Not to be confused with *soutenu.* 2. Bending of the dancer's supporting leg, better called PLIÉ. 3. BATTEMENT *fondu:* a DÉVELOPPÉ performed while bending the supporting leg.

Russian teachers, with their characteristic insistence that movements should be smooth and soft, never sharp or jerky, were so much in the habit of calling out " *Fondu!* " (literal translation : melted) as their pupils made a landing from a jump that with the passage of time the word *fondu* took the place of *plié*, so that dancers were eventually instructed to perform *fondu* (thus making a verb from an adjective) instead of " *Pliez!* " (bend), which latter is in fact what they are doing; just as *raccourci sur le cou-de-pied* and *rotation* have come to be known as *petit fouetté* and *grand fouetté* respectively, because it is the sharpness of the movements which provide the characteristic quality.

FOOT, POSITIONS OF THE.   See also FEET, POSITIONS OF THE; POINTE

FIGURE 82.
PIED À QUART.

FIGURE 83.
PIED À DEMI or SUR LA DEMI-POINTE.

FIGURE 84.
PIED À TROIS QUARTS.

FIGURE 85.
SUR LA POINTE.

Awareness of these positions will help the student; for instance if the dancer wishes to draw one foot up to the knee and raise the heel of the other without turning, the higher he rises the more natural he will find it to pull his body erect, in which position it is easier to balance: whereas turning on the quarter-point is easier because of the larger platform on which the dancer can balance, which is useful at first to give him confidence.

The foot is usually stretched when off the floor.

FOUETTÉ.   See also FONDU ; JETÉ ; BALLONNÉ

I. PETIT.   One leg is extended, and the raised foot whipped in from the knee to the supporting leg and can be done with the supporting leg straight or bent, or after a preparatory jump.

In *petit fouetté* SAUTÉ the dancer springs up raising the right leg to the side: as she lands the right foot is whipped across the left leg, and it is this movement, not the jump, which is accented. *Shortly before the end of the* pas de trois *in " Les Rendezvous " the three dancers perform two* petits fouettés sautés (see illustration p. 2) *on alternate feet followed by an* ASSEMBLÉ *and two* ENTRECHATS QUATRE. *This sequence* (also called COUPÉ-FOUETTÉ RACCOURCI) *is performed four times.*

In *petits fouettés* EN TOURNANT, or FLIC-FLAC, the dancer whips the right foot in across the left leg, flicking the floor as it moves: the body turns to face the back while the right foot remains in the same place and the right leg therefore straightens. The right foot is then whipped across the back of the left leg in the same manner while the dancer completes the turn to face the audience. The effectiveness of the step is created by the smoothness of the turn which contrasts with the sharpness of the foot movement.

Fouetté ROND DE JAMBE EN TOURNANT is generally known simply as *fouetté* and is therefore dealt with here instead of under *rond de jambe*. It consists of a *demi grand rond de jambe en l'air* from the front to the side, and a *petit fouetté* as the dancer turns.

The dancer stands with the right leg raised in front: she throws the right leg around to the side, rising on to the left toe, and whips the right foot in (*fouetté*) to the left knee as she begins to turn. At the completion of one or more turns, if she wishes to turn again in the same manner the dancer quickly extends the right foot to the audience and lowers the left heel, slightly bending the left knee.

FIGURE 86

On her entrance in the coda of the " Black Swan " pas de deux, *Odile performs a series of thirty-two* fouettés *ronds de jambe en* tournant en dehors *(Figure* 86): *and Odette at the end of the* pas de deux *in Act 2 of " Swan Lake " performs a series, interspersed with* petits battements SERRÉS EN PROMENADE *(p.* 39, *Figure* 43), *while supported by Siegfried's finger.*

(*N.B. As Odette is on tiptoe she does not bend the supporting leg between* fouettés.)

2. GRAND or GRAND DÉGAGÉ, better named ROTATION or PIVOTÉ. (See also FONDU.)

One leg is extended in front of the dancer: he turns sharply to face the opposite direction leaving the leg extended behind him. Alternatively if he begins with the leg behind, he then turns to face it (DEDANS).

Grand fouetté can be done by turning the supporting heel on the ground, or rising on to the toe, or during a jump.

The coda of the " Swan Lake" pas de trois begins with one of the female dancers performing seven grands fouettés sautés jumping and beating the legs before turning (grand fouetté SAUTÉ BATTU *or* CABRIOLE fouetté), *on alternate legs. (When the legs are beaten after turning, the term* cabriole ITALIENNE *is used: when they beat before and after turning,* cabriole BECK).

Grands fouettés can also be performed on one leg. The dancer stands on the right leg and throws the left high in front while rising on the right toe. With the impetus thus gained she then makes a half turn with the left leg raised in front of her before performing the *fouetté* movement. This movement can be performed SAUTÉ. When performed in a series it is usual for the dancer to rise on to the toe to steady herself immediately after each complete turn.

The Lilac Fairy concludes her solo in the Prologue of " The Sleeping Beauty" with a series of three grands fouettés turning on the right leg, followed by a turn EN DEDANS: this whole sequence is performed twice before the final bar of her solo.

A *grand fouetté* EN TOURNANT consists of a step backwards on to the left foot turning to face the back before swinging the right leg up in a *grand fouetté*, so that the dancer finishes facing the audience on the left foot, with the right raised behind, having completed a half turn on each leg. This movement can be performed rising on to the toe or with a jump during the *fouetté*.

FRAPPÉ, BATTEMENT. See CLASS (p. 37)

FREE DANCE, CENTRAL EUROPEAN DANCE, BAREFOOT DANCE or *MODERN DANCE*

Originally terms used to describe untrained dancers who performed with the aid of inspiration, not technique. Modern dance as developed in the United States has now become a recognised dance form with a technique or techniques of its own.

At the beginning of the 20th century free dance became popular, together with psychology, free love, the Suffragette movement, jazz, Dadaism, nudism, pacifism, and so forth. Like all of these movements, over the years it has attracted some genuine masters and many bogus exponents and has now become a respectable and scientific logical form with quite as many rules and prejudices as the forms from which it broke away.

At first ballet dancers and " free " dancers would have nothing to do with one another on principle, but today many classical choreographers present works showing that they have learned a great deal from the modern dance movement, while many modern dance companies also have classes in classical ballet.

Today such choreographers as Glen Tetley and John Butler work freely with classical companies, while van Manen, van Dantzig, Morrice and others use many movements from the " modern " vocabulary.

FRENCH METHOD. See METHOD

GARGOUILLADE or ROND DE JAMBE DOUBLÉ

During a jump in the course of which the dancer bends first one leg and then the other up beneath himself, both feet describe little circles in the air.

This movement is frequently made in the course of PAS DE CHAT and of TEMPS DE FLÈCHE, when the steps are then referred to respectively as *gargouillade* and *gargouillade* VOLÉ. It can also be done at the beginning of a CONTRETEMPS, and one of the most striking examples of its use is when it is preceded by an ENVELOPPÉ and followed by a PIROUETTE EN ATTITUDE DEHORS.

At the beginning of the last diagonal of the Dance of the Sugar Plum Fairy, the dancer should perform a pas de chat *with* gargouillade *and* DÉTOURNÉ, *which she repeats three times, then a* POSÉ *into* ARABESQUE *and a* PAS DE BOURRÉE. The whole sequence is performed three times. Many dancers perform simple *pas de chat* without *gargouillade* (p. 71, Figure 96)

GATEWAY, THE. See p. 12, Figure 9

GENOU, LE. See also PLIÉ; ETENDU

The knee. JARRET, the back of the knee.

GLISSADE; GLISSÉ (p. 34); GLISSER (p. 82)

A smooth travelling step gliding along the ground, beginning and ending with the feet together. The knees bend slightly before one leg is extended; then the weight is transferred on to it, when the other closes in to it on bent knees. *Glissades* may also be performed on the tips of the toes and are occasionally performed in class with a beat.

On Giselle's first entrance, immediately after she has run back to her door for the first time, she takes Albrecht's arm and they perform four glissades *before she sits down on the bench.*

During the Betrayed Girl's solo in " The Rake's Progress " she puts down her embroidery and performs six glissades *on her toes* (glissades PRESSÉS).

GRAND

Big, large. The converse of PETIT. I. Differentiates between large and small varieties of the same step. 2. Distinguishes between two varieties of the same type of movement.

GRECQUE, ATTITUDE. See ARMS, POSITIONS OF THE (p. 13 ; Figure 13)

GUEST ARTIST, PERMANENT. See p. 5

HANDS, POSITION OF THE

Each system has slightly differing ideas on the correct manner in which the dancer should hold his hands, Blasis, Cecchetti and the R.A.D. employing set positions for the student. The positions for the student at the *barre* are designed to prevent straining and stretching of the fingers, and these positions become relaxed more naturally when dancing.

FIGURE 87.
Blasis hand position and
R.A.D. *Barre.*

FIGURE 88.
CECCHETTI, *Barre*
position.

FIGURE 89.
FRENCH METHOD,
Barre position.

In all systems the hands are generally intended to be slightly rounded in continuation of the arm, except in *arabesque* positions: Vaganova directs that the hands be sometimes allowed to trail after the arms when they descend to give a floating appearance. When the arms are straight, the hands take a more stiff position in accordance with the more direct line of the arm, when both are said to be EXTENDED.

HAUT, EN. See p. 13, Figures 19, 21

HAUTEUR, À LA. See LEG, POSITIONS OF THE

HEAD, POSITIONS OF THE. See also CLASS (p. 41); SPOTTING

Awareness of the possible varieties in the use of the head helps the dancer to avoid monotony of presentation.

(*N.B.* When the head is held " erect " the chin is slightly raised to enable the face to catch the stage lights, most of which come from above.)

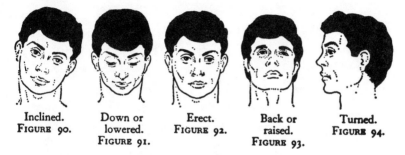

Inclined.	Down or	Erect.	Back or	Turned.
FIGURE 90.	lowered.	FIGURE 92.	raised.	FIGURE 94.
	FIGURE 91.		FIGURE 93.	

HORTENSIA. See also PASSÉ

The dancer stands with the feet apart, one in front of the other, springs up and changes the legs one, two or three times in the manner of a swimmer performing the " crawl," landing with the feet apart. There is no suggestion of a beat about this step.

The leading male dancer of " Les Patineurs " comes to the centre of the stage and performs this step twice to open his variation (Figure 95).

FIGURE 95   FIGURE 96

ITALIAN METHOD. See METHOD

JAMBE, OUVERTURE DE

A GRAND ROND DE JAMBE EN L'AIR executed as quickly as possible.

JAMBE, POSITIONS DE. See LEG, POSITIONS OF THE;
RONDS DE. See CLASS (p. 35) ; FOUETTÉ ;
GARGOUILLADE

JARRET. See GENOU, LE *JARRETÉ.* See ARQUÉ

JETÉ. See also SISSONE; BASQUE, SAUT DE; BALLOTTÉ; POSE

There are three basic types of *jeté*, with many variations. 1. GRAND *jeté*; 2. *Jeté* A LA SECONDE; 3. *Jeté* PASSÉ; (See also PIQUÉ, POSÉ)
All are jumps from one leg to the other.

1. GRAND *jeté* EN AVANT. With the right leg raised in front, the dancer springs up and forward, landing on the right foot, the left leg held either straight or bent EN ATTITUDE behind him. This *jeté* is usually preceded by one or more steps to provide greater impetus, but this is not invariable.

On his entrance, the Spirit of the Rose stands on the window-sill and then does a GLISSADE *followed by a* grand jeté en avant, *looking back and downwards to soften the leap* (*Figure* 97).

To begin the coda of the "Black Swan" pas de deux, Siegfried enters in a series of grands jetés en avant (*Figure* 99), *interspersed with* PAS COURU, *travelling round the stage* (EN MANÈGE).

GRAND PAS DE CHAT. As *grand jeté en avant*, except that the knee thrown out in front is bent during the jump.

Grand jeté en avant BATTU. As the dancer springs (as in a *grand jeté en avant*) he brings the front leg straight beneath the body, beating away the back leg which rises behind him as he lands.

COUPÉ *jeté* EN TOURNANT. A *coupé* under, executed while making three-quarters of a turn on bent legs, followed by a *grand jeté en avant*, commonly called *coupé jeté*.

The dancer's left leg is extended behind, and the right slightly bent: the dancer *coupés*, i.e. brings the raised leg quickly in to replace the right which rises until the foot touches the left shin; simultaneously the dancer turns bending the knees still further. Then with the impetus thus gained the dancer performs a *jeté*, shooting the right leg high out in front and jumping straight on to it, while the back leg is either straight, or bent *en attitude*.

To end his solo in the "Swan Lake" pas de trois, the male dancer performs twelve coupés jetés en tournant *round the stage* (*see* title-page).

It is possible to execute *coupés jetés en tournant* turning on the *jeté* instead of the *coupé*, but this is rare.

TOUR DE REINS. Also called COUPÉ-CHASSÉ-COUPÉ-JETÉ. A compound step composed of four movements: *a. Coupé* under, turning with a jump; *b.* CHASSÉ forward; *c. Coupé* under turning with bent knees; *d. Grand jeté en avant.*

FIGURE 97

FIGURE 98

FIGURE 99

Grand jeté can be performed EN ARRIÈRE by raising the foot behind and springing backwards on to it, but is comparatively rare as no impetus can be gained by a preparatory run.

Grand jeté can also be performed sideways (DE COTÉ).

Billy ends his Soliloquy in " Billy the Kid" by performing a jeté de côté, FERMÉ, and the movement is repeated during the course of the ballet (p. 73, Figure 98).

Grand jeté FOUETTÉ or *jeté passé en avant en tournant* begins as does an ordinary GRAND JETÉ EN facing the direction from which he began (*fouetté* DEDANS). Throwing the right leg in front, the dancer springs forward off the left, and at the height of the jump turns his body sharply to the left, to face in the opposite direction, landing with the left leg raised in front of him.

In the second movement of " Interplay," immediately after the leading male dancer has been joined by two girls for the second time, he leaves the second girl (pretending to be shocked at her repetition of his " hula" movement) to jump straight into a jeté fouetté, which is repeated during the course of a big sweep round the stage (Figure 100).

FIGURE 100

2. JETÉ À LA SECONDE. To perform a series of these *jetés* the dancer begins with the right foot raised and touching the left calf As he bends the left leg the right foot brushes out to the side and continues to rise as he jumps. On descending he lands on the right leg, drawing the left up to touch the other calf.

Jeté BATTEMENT or *Jeté* PETIT *battement.* This is not a jumping step and is seldom seen on the stage. The right leg is bent, the left foot touching the back of the right ankle. The left is brought round to the front, then whipped out to the side; as the left closes in front, the right is drawn up behind it with a slight hop to recommence the movement to the other side.

To perform *jeté battement* EN ARRIÈRE the left leg commences in front and is taken to the back of the right ankle before extending. *Jeté* ROND DE JAMBE is a *jeté à la seconde* followed by a *rond de jambe en l'air sauté*.

3. JETÉ PASSÉ: or, if the knees are bent, JETÉ EN ATTITUDE, also called EMBOÎTÉ. The dancer stands with the right leg behind him, then springs, passing his legs in mid-air to land on the right foot with the left leg behind him. The dancer may beat his calves together in the air just before the legs pass. These *jetés* can also be done with the legs raised in front (EN AVANT).

Grand jeté en attitude is a feature of Albrecht's solo in Act 2 of " Giselle " (p. 76, Figure 102).

The four cygnets in Act 2 of " Swan Lake " conclude their dance with sixteen little jetés en attitude in groups of four, alternating to front and back. Earlier in the dance they perform a series of 32 alternating in the same manner.

An effect of added lightness is given to *jeté en attitude* by the addition of a CHASSÉ. After the *jeté* the dancer slides the back raised leg in front of him before commencing another *jeté* off the same leg. This combination is usually referred to as STEP-JETÉ but is also called PAS DE PAPILLON and PAS DE CHAT.

PETIT *jeté* or EMBOÎTÉ. The dancer stands on the right foot with the left touching the right ankle in front. He springs up and brings the right foot in front, to land with it touching the left ankle. This can also be done DERRIÈRE, lifting the foot behind the other ankle. *Petits jetés* are usually performed making a half turn in the same direction on each jump (EN TOURNANT).

Before the DEMI-TOURS which conclude Petipa's arrangement of Aurora's solo in the Vision Scene, Aurora performs a series of eight petits jetés en tournant (p. 76, Figure 101).

GRAND *jeté* DESSUS EN TOURNANT or *jeté* PEREKIDNOY or *jeté* ENTRELACÉE or TOUR *jeté*. This step is either a *grand jeté en avant* or a *jeté passé* or a *grand jeté de côté* performed while turning in the air. The dancer stands with the right leg extended behind him. Turning his back, he steps on to the right leg (now before him) and bends it, at the same time throwing his left leg past high into the air, and springs, raising his arms to help himself. While he is in the air the dancer turns to the front again changing his legs so that he lands on the left leg in the position in which he began, with his arms extended at the side of his shoulders.

This step may be performed BATTU, the dancer beating his legs once as they pass, or beating the right leg beneath the left, changing them and beating again before raising the right and landing on the left.

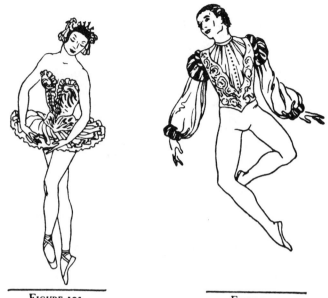

FIGURE 101   FIGURE 102

The male dancer in the pas de trois *from " Swan Lake " opens his
solo with a* chassé, coupé, chassé *travelling backwards and a* grand
jeté en avant dessus en tournant. *This* jeté *recurs three times.*
(For another example see CABRIOLE.)

JETÉ ENVELOPPÉ

This step is the same as a *saut de basque (q.v.),* except that the *grand
battement en avant* is performed in *attitude.*

JUPONNAGE. See TUTU

KIT. See preface; *KNEE HEIGHT.* See CLASS (p. 36);
KNOCK KNEES. See ARQUÉ

LEÇON. See CLASS

LEG, POSITIONS OF THE. See also FEET, POSITIONS
OF THE; FOOT, POSITIONS OF THE

The illustrations on the opposite page are given with the leg at
the side (À LA SECONDE), in a stationary position but it may be
at the back (À LA QUATRIÈME DERRIÈRE or EN ARABESQUE) or
front (À LA QUATRIÈME DEVANT) and when the dancer is in the air
the supporting leg may provide no level of comparison. If the leg

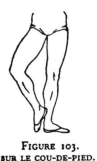

FIGURE 103.
SUR LE COU-DE-PIED.

FIGURE 104.
ATTITUDE À
TERRE.

FIGURE 105.
DEMI-RETIRÉ or
DEMI-RACCOURCI.

FIGURE 106.
RETIRÉ or RACCOURCI
or EN TIRE-BOUCHON
or PASSÉ POSITION.

FIGURE 107.
POINTE TENDUE or
PIQUÉ À TERRE or DÉGAGÉ.

FIGURE 108.
DÉGAGÉ or
TENDUE.

FIGURE 109.
DEMI or À LA DEMI-
HAUTEUR or 45°.

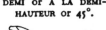

FIGURE 110.
GRAND or EN L'AIR.

FIGURE 111.
À LA HAUTEUR
or 90°.

FIGURE 112.
EXTENDED (any position
considerably above hip level).

is bent in Figures 107 to 112 it is in ATTITUDE at that height.

An " extended " position looks beautiful in dancers of the *jarreté* type loose enough to sustain it without strain—therefore said to have " a good extension ". The dancing of Eva Evdokimova is full of quite extraordinary extensions.

77

LEOTARD

This garment was invented in the middle of the 19th century by the French acrobat Jules Leotard, the first man to use the flying trapeze. Basically it is a tightly fitting garment covering the body from wrists to ankle: many varieties are used to-day, both in the practice room—where it has the double advantage of at once keeping the limbs warm and revealing every line of the body—and on the stage, either without ornamentation for the many " practice dress " ballets in vogue to-day or decorated as in Sidney Nolan's costumes for " The Rite of Spring " (Macmillan).

LIFTS. See ENLÈVEMENT

LIGNE or LINE

A term loosely adapted from painting. Every group and position on the stage should, like a painting, have a dominant line supplemented, either by contrast or parallel, by the other lines. No painter would begin a picture without having its main shape in mind: so all painters have a considerable knowledge of line and its endless varieties, unlike most dancers who find a few favourite ways of placing themselves, and always affect that manner whatever the role. This soon becomes boring.

Straight legs and arms can make a pose very restless if they all point in different directions, but if they all lead in one direction (or are complementary to it) a great impression of clarity results. Likewise if one curved line is aided by complementary lines a restfulness will appear: whereas if there are many curved lines sprouting in all directions the eye will quickly weary of the incoherence.

Considerable effect can be made by breaking a harmonious position by flicking the hand or head out of line, but this should only be used sparingly.

Massine's gift for portraying innumerable different characters, each with their individual and distinctive line, demonstrates the potentialities of many different kinds of line and is doubtless due to his great interest in painting.

LIMBERING. See CLASS (p. 40)

LYRE, EN. See p. 13, Figure 17

MAILLOT. See TIGHTS

MAIN, MAINS. See HANDS, POSITIONS OF THE

MAÎTRE, MAÎTRESSE DE BALLET

In ballet's early days when choreographer meant " dance notator," the *maître de ballet* was the arranger of the dances. To-day the term is used to designate the person responsible for rehearsing ballets in the repertory, for taking daily classes and occasionally for casting, which latter task is frequently performed by the director or artistic director of the company or even the choreographer.

MANÈGE, EN or AUTOUR DE LA SALLE

Indicates that steps are performed by the dancer travelling in a circle round the stage. (See PIROUETTE ; BASQUE, PAS DE ; JETÉ.)

MARCHÉ, PAS.   See PAS MARCHÉ

MARCHEUSE or FIGURANTE.   See FIGURANTE

MARQUER

Indicates that: 1. The dancer accentuates a step; 2. That at rehearsal he sketches out the movements of a dance without any energy, or marks out with his hands what his legs should be doing

METHOD or SCHOOL or STYLE; FRENCH, ITALIAN, RUSSIAN AND DANISH

No two teachers teach exactly alike but all profess to follow some method, the above four being the important ones.

During the 16th and 17th centuries, the French co-ordinated ballet from a medley of steps into a scientific technique; this accounts for the use of French in the technical language of ballet. The French concentrated on what could then be seen—brilliant footwork and elegant elaborate arm movements.   Camargo appeared in Paris *circa* 1730 in heelless shoes and a skirt cut off just below the calf (which created a scandal), to show the full brilliance of that technique, and by 1759 Noverre was anxious to reform some of the methods of the French school which had already become set in its ways.

After the French Revolution (1789) new laws were needed to suit new ideas and conditions; these laws were modelled on those of the Republics of Greece and Rome as they seemed most suitable to current events; so everything, including painting, fashions of dress, opera and ballet followed suit in an orgy of pseudo-Classic art.   The resulting freedom of dress naturally allowed full and unrestricted use of the limbs, and the new Milanese school took immediate advantage of this and laid the accent on technique.   Consequently the Italian method was formed by virtuosi who developed ballet throughout the 19th century into the comprehensive instrument it is to-day.

During most of the 19th century the Italian dancers headed foreign companies dazzling the world with their feats, even in St. Petersburg, which had supported a State Ballet school under French masters since 1735.

Petipa, a very diplomatic man, was in command there from 1862 until the early 20th century. Petipa, who came of a dancing family, loved the elegance of the French school in which he had been brought up, and which suited his physique so well; therefore while he had to satisfy the current thirst for virtuosity in his ballets he always contrived to use this for a beautiful purpose, changing the accent once again to elegance. This change has given rise to the Russian school which has been developing along these lines ever since, with Italian brilliance and French elegance to spur it on.

From the foregoing the reader will have gathered that the Italian or Milanese school, with its interest in technique, was dominated by the powerful ARQUÉ dancers, whereas the Soviet school is personified by the elegant JARRETÉ.

Arqués and *jarretés* have contrasting abilities and drawbacks and one can therefore see how wise it is for the former to embrace the Italian method, exemplified by Cecchetti, which was formed around their physical type, and the latter to embrace the Russian, exemplified by Vaganova, for the same reason. It should also become evident that a new school to suit every dancer, containing all the good points of every other and none of the bad, is a pipe dream. What is now necessary is the clarification of the Italian and Russian methods, with the two physiques that their aims happened to require in the forefront of the mind, so that one will no longer see dancers trying to dance with the aid of methods which suit their idols or their teachers but not themselves.

Oddly enough, the place in which to see the purest example today of the authentic " French school " is in Denmark, where the Bournonville tradition has preserved the style of Vestris in a practically untouched state : while the " Russian style " holds sway in Paris through the influence of the great teachers Kchessinskaya, Preobrajenska and Egorova and their pupils.

It is typical of the ingenious and analytical mind of Antony Tudor that he could make the essential difference between the three balletic styles the subject of a ballet, " Gala Performance," which in the original production with Maude Lloyd, Peggy van Praagh and Gerd Larsen held the audience despite the fact that the majority of them did not appreciate the essential differentiation : which was the most fascinating ingredient of the work to the trained dancer, whether observing or performing in it. Unfortunately, the ballet does not seem to be cast today with this in mind, but merely " played for laughs," thus making nonsense of the whole thing, and turning what was originally a work of great style and beauty into an irritating romp.

MILIEU, AU. See CLASS (p. 41)

MIME or, occasionally, *PANTOMIME*

Generally used to describe both the narrative passages in the classical ballets and the stylised gestures used in such passages. Perhaps the best known example is that of Odette's explanation to Siegfried in Act 2 of " Swan Lake." Conventional mime is almost entirely manual and, like the deaf and dumb finger language which it curiously resembles, presupposes a familiarity with its symbolic meaning on the spectator's part. Nevertheless, when practised by a great artist such as Karsavina or Wolkonsky, conventional mime acquires a singular beauty and significance. The artist projects himself instinctively to the spectator who succumbs to a dreamlike, almost hypnotic experience.

Nowadays the truly creative choreographer uses themes which can be expressed entirely in terms of movement, and therefore need no programme notes or complicated formal mime sequences.

Mime as cultivated independently in Paris to-day is quite distinct from balletic mime. The trained ballet dancer will always use his basic technique as a foundation upon which to build the character he seeks to portray, whereas the French mime appears to be completely fluid and his essential movement to alter radically in accordance with the character or nature of the thing he endeavours to become. This is achieved by a system of balance and counter-balance, and a complete control of each individual muscle; this control is effected almost entirely from the diaphragm.

Within the confines of the balletic form, Tudor, Jooss, and Robbins are particularly notable among present-day choreographers for their attempts to invent new movements which will convey their meaning to the spectator.

MIME, A. See also BALLERINA, PRIMA; MIME

One who mimes. Western dancers are not taught by actors and this makes the performance of such outstanding mimes as Emblen, Grant and Hayworth most remarkable. However, even these artists cannot equal Russian mimes such as Radunsky, Lapauri, Levashov and Gridin.

MIRROR DANCER

Disparaging term used by dancers for those who have unfortunately been allowed for years to practise every exercise staring into the mirrors covering the walls of many ballet studios. The bad effects of this habit are two : First, that the dancer even at performance continues to gaze forward with a lost expression towards where his mirror used to be—now replaced by a large black space containing the audience ; secondly, this eternal searching for the dancer's own reflection means that his partner never sees his face and so can obtain no contact with him, even when the pair may be enacting the rôles of lovers.

Jerome Robbins in his " L'Après-midi d'un Faune " makes both his dancers look into the mirror most of the time even when they are practising a *pas de deux*—the " mirror " in question being, of course, the large black space containing the audience referred to above. This gives the ballet a strange and fascinating impersonality and demonstrates the narcissism which often results from hours of practice alone, as well as demonstrating the choreographer's main point—that, despite very close physical proximity, dancers have little idea of what are the thoughts and feelings of their fellow-workers.

MODERN DANCE. See FREE DANCE

MODIFICATIONS

Qualifying terms, for example EN TOURNANT, BATTU, ALLONGÉ, COLLÉ, etc., used to indicate to the dancer in which way he should execute a given step, or take up a position.

MONTER. See RELEVÉ

MOVEMENTS, CAMRYN'S 20 BASIC CHARACTERS. See CHARACTER DANCER

MOVEMENTS IN DANCING, 7

Students are taught that there are seven movements in dancing: PLIER (to bend), ÉTENDRE (to stretch), RELEVER (to rise), SAUTER (to jump), ÉLANCER (to dart), GLISSER (to glide), TOURNER (to turn). This classification enables them to analyse steps more easily and give clarity to their efforts, vague as the terms may be.

NARRATIVE BALLET. See CLASSICAL BALLET

NATIONAL DANCING: NATIONAL BALLET.
See CHARACTER DANCING and INTRODUCTION respectively

NOTATION. See also CHOREOGRAPHER; PATTERN

For over five hundred years attempts have been made to write down dances, but no system so far devised has received universal acceptance: although from the great activity and interest shown in this field since Laban and Margaret Morris published their two systems independently in 1928, and the current use of systems to record dances here and in America, it seems that the notation of ballet may come into its own. This is greatly to be desired, as the choreographer, unlike artists in other media, cannot now refer to past masters, and to realise how great a handicap this can be one has only to imagine how hopeless would have been the struggles of Beethoven without the example of Haydn from which to learn, those of Dali without the example of Bosch.

If dance notation were universally learned and accepted it would then matter little if choreography were altered by different hands for each performance, for the original would still exist.

OPERA BALLET

In the operas of Rameau and Lully, the ballet, while in no way forming an integral part of the operatic plot, was the *raison d'être* of the performance, and only under the influence of Gluck did opera-ballet take its rightful secondary place and begin to be used as a dramatic component of the whole performance. Towards the end of the 19th century a ballet (conventionally inserted into the second act of an opera) became virtually obligatory, presumably to keep the spectators awake or the opera dancers at work, and this ballet was either a vital part of the opera as in " Prince Igor," " Samson and Delilah " or " Ballo in Maschera," or was in no way connected with it, and could be omitted without harming either continuity or musical form.

To-day the creation of opera ballet presents the choreographer with an interesting problem, for this type of ballet offers him a half-way home between ballets of which the music was composed specially for the choreographer, and ballets arranged in the current fashion of grafting dances on to music not originally intended for ballet: in most cases the composer is long since dead and there can be no question of collaboration between the two artists, whereas on the other hand the music was composed with ballet—and ballet localised in time, place and plot—in mind.

It is useless for the choreographer of opera-ballets to attack his problem purely from the balletic angle, as if he does so the dancing may present an incongruous appearance: he is subject to the ideas of the composer, to the style of dancing required according to the locale of the opera, and the wishes of the current producer. However, if he can surpass all these obstacles the finished result can produce an effect possibly more cumulatively satisfying to the spectator than that produced by any other form of ballet, as is the case when the dancers join the singers at the end of Act 2 of "Prince Igor" as arranged by Fokine, and in Heinz Rosen's production of Carl Orff's "Trionfi".

OPERATIC DANCER.   See also FIGURANTE

Term first used by Édouard Espinosa in 1897 to replace "ballet dancer" which at that time bore unflattering connotations. This attempt to render the profession a respectable one in England was completed by his pupil, Dame Ninette de Valois.

OPPOSITION.   See also DIRECTIONS (p. 52)

A relationship of the arms to the legs discussed at length by Noverre and Blasis; based on the action of walking and therefore considered the most natural method of balancing the body. When the dancer's right leg is in front and left leg behind, he puts his arms into *opposition* by raising the left arm in front of him, taking the right to the side or back: the reverse of OUVERT arms.

Opposition arm positions occur in Figures 50, 54, 62, 99, 126, 127

OUVERT(E).   See also DIRECTIONS (p. 52)

1. A position of the arms in which the dancer stands with his right leg in front and left leg behind, raising his right arm in front and taking the left to the side or back, as in Figures 2, 24, 33, 36, 49, 57, 59, 86, 97, 100 ; the reverse of OPPOSITION arms.
2. A position of the feet in which the feet do not touch. The 2nd, 4th and Lifar's 7th positions are *ouverte*; the reverse of FERMÉ.

PANTOMIME.   See MIME

PAPILLON, PAS DE.   See JETÉ EN ATTITUDE (p. 75)

PAR TERRE.   See TERRE, À

PARTNERING or PAS DE DEUX.   See DOUBLE WORK

PAS

Step or dance.   When used in conjunction with French numerals, indicates the number of dancers concerned: i.e., a *pas seul* is a solo, *pas de deux* a dance for two, *pas de trois* a dance for three, and so on up to *pas de huit,* or dance for eight dancers. It is also used on the programme to indicate who is to dance, i.e. " *Pas des Patineuses* " in " Les Patineurs." The *grand pas de deux* for the ballerina and her partner was regarded as the climax of the type of ballet from which Fokine revolted in Russia early in this century.

PAS ALLÉ

The dancer appears to walk quite naturally on the stage, unlike PAS MARCHÉ.

PAS COURU. See also COURSE, PAS DE

Running steps.

The GRAND JETÉS EN AVANT *performed by Siegfried in the coda of the " Black Swan "* pas de deux *(p. 73, Figure 99) are interspersed with* pas courus.

PAS DE BOURRÉES *courus* were once better described as PETITS *pas courus.*

PAS MARCHÉ

The dancer walks in a stylised manner, forcing the feet in front and bringing each foot out to the side as it passes the other: a relic of the days when noblemen wore elaborate high boots, making it difficult to pass the legs close together, and considered dancing an essential social accomplishment.

PASSÉ

Added to the name of a step means: 1. That the extended leg is passed from the front to the back (or vice versa), as in DEVELOPPÉ SAUTÉ *passé* and CHASSÉ *passé.* Examples will be found under ÉCHAPPÉ and SISSONE. 2. That the dancer lands on one leg and, as it bends, swings the other through to the back as in GRAND PAS DE BASQUE *passé,* also called PAS CISEAUX, GRAND BATTEMENT SAUTÉ *passé,* HORTENSIA *passé.* 3. That one foot is picked up and brought round in front of (or behind) the other as in RETIRÉ *passé* and SISSONE SIMPLE *passé.*

Both *grands battements en arrière sautés passés* and *developpés passés en arrière* are sometimes called PASSÉS or TEMPS DE FLÉCHE.

(*N.B.* Because a series of RETIRÉS FERMÉS are usually performed *passés* at the barre, retirés are frequently called simply *passés* even when the foot does not change from the back to the front or vice versa.)

PATTERN or FLOOR PATTERN

Although groups in ballet should have a clear pattern when seen from the stalls, pattern in ballet invariably means the lines in which the dancers stand or the lines in which they move on the stage as seen from above. This is one of the beauties of " Les Sylphides " which is entirely lost from the stalls, though its effect is felt even there because the dancers appear to travel with some purpose.

Old systems of dance notation were based on tracing the pattern made on the floor by the dancer, and nowadays when dancers jot down a part to help themselves it is usually the floor pattern, with the names of a few key steps, that they commit to paper.

Those who saw " Choreartium " or " The Wanderer " will never forget the patterns of the dancers' movements, particularly in the second movement of the former ballet. On the other hand there are ballets such as " Taras Bulba " and " Danses Concertantes " which are more effective from the stalls.

PENCHÉ. See ARABESQUE; ATTITUDE; BAISSÉ

PETIT. See GRAND; PETIT BATTEMENT. See CLASS (p. 37); PETIT SUJET. See BALLERINA, PRIMA; PETIT TOURS. See TOURS, DEMI

PIED. See FOOT, POSITIONS OF THE; PIEDS. See FEET POSITIONS OF THE; PIEDS DANS LA MAIN. See CLASS (p. 41)

PIEDS, CHANGEMENTS DE. See also RETIRÉ

The dancer springs up, straightening the knees in the air, and changes the feet before landing, the feet land together in the reverse position. These jumps resemble *sauts* and *soubresauts*. *Changements* become ENTRECHATS once a beating of the legs is added.

PIGEON, TEMPS DE, or PIGEON, AILES DE or FAILLI FERMÉ. See also PISTOLET

The dancer springs into the air, bending the back leg slightly behind the front one and beating the legs at the height of the jump. He then alights on the front foot, leaving the back foot tucked up behind the ankle, and then immediately bringing the back foot round to the front and closing it in fifth position.
During the course of Harlequin's " Paganini " Variation, which closes with the pirouette *described on p. 88, the dancer should perform a series of temps de pigeon in the front left-hand corner of the stage, but owing to its extreme difficulty this step is often replaced by a series of* RETIRÉS *over on a* RELEVÉ.

PIQUÉ.   See also BOURRÉE, PAS DE; PIROUETTE; POSÉ

1. The dancer steps sharply on to one toe without bending the same knee. Also called JETÉ SUR LA POINTE.
2. A step performed in staccato fashion.
3. A movement in which the feet are picked up sharply.

PIQUÉ À TERRE.   See LEG, POSITIONS OF THE

PIROUETTE or *TOUR.*   See also SPOTTING; TOURS, DEMI

A turn on one leg, in which the dancer spins round on one foot; performed EN DEDANS or EN DEHORS (see page 54).

Pirouettes are at first performed with the raised foot touching the other leg (p. 89, Figure 115); later the student learns to perform them with the raised leg extended, in which case the movements are termed *pirouettes* EN ARABESQUE, *pirouettes* À LA SECONDE, *pirouettes* EN ATTITUDE EN AVANT, etc.

Occasionally during *pirouettes* the dancer may execute RONDS DE JAMBE EN L'AIR, BATTEMENTS FRAPPÉS or PETITS BATTEMENTS.

Sometimes a dancer will begin to turn in one position and continue in another.

A RENVERSÉ movement of the body can also be performed while executing *pirouettes*, generally during the last turn.

The dancer always *pirouettes* on the toe; when he lowers his heel and rises again at the completion of each spin in a series, he is performing a RELEVÉ *pirouette*.

The most comfortable way in which to prepare for a *pirouette* is by standing evenly on both feet.

The third solo in the pas de trois *from " Swan Lake " concludes with a series of* piqués pirouettes en dehors *(Figure 115), with* coupés *so that the turns are all on the same leg.*

The second Blue Girl in " Les Patineurs " commences her solo with two single piqués pirouettes en dedans *followed by a double* piqué pirouette en attitude en dedans *(Figure 114) during which alternate arms are raised above the head. This sequence is repeated travelling round the stage* (EN MANÈGE).

SAUTÉS PIROUETTES.   *Sautés pirouettes* is a rather misleading term, as the dancer does not jump, but spins round with one leg raised: pivoting on the ball of the foot he quickly shifts the heel round in tiny sharp movements, causing the leg and body to revolve (Figure 113).

As the curtain falls on " Les Patineurs " the male dancer is performing sautés pirouettes a la seconde *alone on the stage.*

After Giselle's entrance in Act 2, she bows to Myrtha (p. 9 Fig. 3) and then rises straight into a series of sautés pirouettes en arabesque.

GRAND PIROUETTE. An exercise based on *sautés* and *relevés pirouettes à là seconde*, of which there are many variations.

Harlequin concludes his " Paganini " variation in " Carnaval " with a grand pirouette *consisting of* sautés *(Figure* 113) *and* relevés pirouettes à la seconde *followed by a* pirouette *with the right foot on the left knee* (RETIRÉ) *before sitting down in the centre of the stage.*

SUPPORTED PIROUETTES are a part of double work where the male dancer steadies his partner as she spins.

PISTOLET or AILES DE PIGEON. See also PIGEON, TEMPS DE

The dancer throws the left leg up, springing off the right which rises to beat beneath the left calf: the legs change and beat again, and change once more for the dancer to land leaving the left leg extended in the air. Because of the extreme difficulty of this step when performed EN AVANT or EN ARRIÈRE, it is common, after throwing the leg up and springing, to beat first on top of the raised leg: then to change the legs and beat again so that the right leg is already beneath for the dancer to land on. However, the more complicated beat is not unknown, Peter Schaufuss in particular performing it superbly.

The male dancer in the " Blue Bird " variation after his preliminary TEMPS LEVÉ CHASSÉ PASSÉ *throws his left leg in front to execute* pistolet en avant, *which sequence is performed twice more travelling diagonally (Figure* 116). *This step is sometimes omitted nowadays and the solo cut by nearly a third, which of course makes it possible to to give an encore.*

PIVOT. See PROMENADE; PIVOTÉ. See FOUETTÉ

PLACE, SUR

A step or sequence of steps performed on the spot.

The " thirty-two fouettés " *in Act* 3 *of " Swan Lake " (p.* 67, *Figure* 86) *should be performed* sur place.

PLACING

A dancer is said to have good placing or to be well placed when the turn-out of the hips, rounded arms and other qualities as taught in ballet class appear natural to her. Without a suitable physique and a first-class teacher such appearance is unlikely.

PLANÉ

Used to qualify those steps in which the dancer attempts to create the illusion that he stops for a moment in mid-air. This may account for the occasional use of TEMPS *plané* for TEMPS DE L'ANGE.

FIGURE 113

FIGURE 114

FIGURE 115

FIGURE 116

PLIÉ or *PLIER LE GENOU*. See also ACHILLES
TENDON; CLASS (p. 33); ELEVATION; ÉTENDU

A bending of the knee or knees (p. 56, Figure 64) used as preparation for most steps, sometimes called FONDU when one of the dancer's legs is extended (Figures 3, 26, 36, 46, 61, 62, 86, 113, 117).

POINTE. See also FOOT, POSITIONS OF THE ; TAQUETÉ

A dancer is on point (" SUR LA *pointe* ") when she is standing or dancing on the tips of her toes. This feat is generally facilitated by the use of specially blocked shoes which leave room for her to pad her toes with cotton wool.

An interesting theory on the origin of the *pointe* shoe was put to us by Kurt Jooss. It is said that Taglioni had the natural faculty of dancing on the extreme tips of her toes in the unblocked ballet slipper of the time; as Taglioni was the most celebrated dancer of her day, shoe-makers were implored by her jealous rivals to fabricate something by which other dancers would be enabled to do likewise: hence the development of the *pointe* or " toe " shoe.

The use of *pointes* grew to be such a mania that no subject, theme or setting was safe from it until Michel Fokine, seventy years after Taglioni's heyday, revolted against ballet's submission to unreality in this attitude, among others, and produced such ballets as " Schéhérazade," " Daphnis and Chloe " and " Thamar " without deference to the *pointe* tradition. Even in " The Firebird " and " Petrouchka " the only dancers to use *pointes* are the Firebird and the Doll—both inhuman creatures to whose movements the *pointes* added a touch of fantasy—and the two street performers in " Petrouchka " where the use of *pointes* was valid to give a suggestion of acrobacy.

The thoughtless use of *pointes* for *pointes'* sake unfortunately prevails even to the present day, encouraged doubtless by the proneness of the audience to greet any ballet not employing *pointe* shoes with the cry of " It's not a ballet."

Occasionally male dancers dance on their *pointes*, for example Dolin in " Les Fâcheux " and " The Fair at Sorochinsk " (Lichine), and Georgian dancers.

In 1952, as a result of a long and bitter crusade by conscientious teachers and an intensive campaign in the American magazines "Dance " and " Dance News," the foremost makers of theatrical shoes in the U.S.A., Capezio's, announced that they would no longer manufacture point shoes for children below the age of eight, a lead that was soon followed by other shoemakers. This is still too young : but that such a campaign should have been necessary shows the appalling ignorance still common apropos the dangers to children's health of too early point work. Despite the persistent insistence by responsible bodies—and in particular by " The Dancing Times "—on the dangers of putting tiny children on their toes, there are still in existence many irresponsible and ignorant teachers who still tell children of four and five to buy point shoes and put them on their toes at their very first lesson.

Many small children attending their first ballet class at the age of seven or eight are bitterly disappointed because nobody " stands on her toes." If these children understood how difficult, uncomfortable and frequently painful point work can be, they would be in less of a hurry to undertake it. But, part of the professional dancer's aim being to avoid showing that what she is doing is not perfectly natural and easy, children who have seen ballet in the theatre or on television gain the impression that all there is to it is simply to rise on the tips of the toes and comfortably remain there, dancing.

In fact, the practise of dancing on point is unnatural, uncomfortable and frequently painful, as anyone can bear witness who has seen a dancer remove her point shoes after a hard class, with the toes covered in blood. Moreover, the problems of balance are radically altered when dancing on the toes—this is obvious to anyone who has noticed a young girl trying to walk down the street in her first pair of high heels : and in that case the heel is supported and the weight taken, not on the extreme tips of the toes, but on the ball of the foot.

It is highly dangerous to attempt point work until the dancer's body is physically ready to begin it, and this should never be attempted before the child is at least eleven years old, because at this age the soft bone-structure has hardened. Even when a child's bones have set, she should not be allowed to begin point work unless she can perform *échappés*, *sous-sous* and *retirés* with the knees straight, the ankles firm, and the back quite straight without bottom or stomach protruding. This last is important, since if the child cannot yet control her spine into one straight line, permanent damage to the back may occur if she is allowed on point.

One cannot help feeling that there was a great deal of truth in the old saying that no dancer should begin point work until she can perform every movement correctly off point, because only when this is so can she safely deal with the problem of carrying the entire weight of the body on the tips of the toes, whereby tension is comfortably dealt with and the chance of physical injury is as slight as possible.

POINTE TENDUE. See LEG, POSITIONS OF THE

POISSON. See also SOUBRESAUT

A position of the body in which the dancer arches her back, lifts her head, and bends back her legs with the feet crossed. This pose may be sustained while jumping as in SOUBRESAUT *poisson* (or TEMPS DE *poisson* (p. 101, Figure 123)), or in double work when the girl is supported in this position and the term PAS *poisson* or FISH DIVE is used.

The " Aurora " grand pas de deux concludes with a fish dive from the shoulder; Aurora also concludes three of her pirouettes in this position (Figure 118).

At the end of her little solo in the finale of " Coppélia," Swanilda springs up on to her partner's shoulder in a fish dive.

PORT DE BRAS. See CLASS (p. 41)

PORTÉ

1. A step is travelled. 2. A girl is carried through the air by her partner (p. 60, Figures 68 and 69).

PORTEUR

A term first used by audiences and critics during the latter half of the 19th century as a sarcastic comment on the activities of the average male dancer who did no dancing by merely carried or supported his partner round the stage.

POSÉ or GRAND DÉGAGÉ or JETÉ SUR LA POINTE or PIQUÉ DÉVELOPPÉ. See also POSER

The manner in which a dancer steps into a position with a small DÉVELOPPÉ. The dancer lifts one foot, bending the knee. He then straightens the leg and steps out on to the toe, raising the supporting leg into a position.

The Sugar Plum Fairy enters for her variation in " The Nutcracker " performing posés (Figure 117).

POSER or STEP or POSÉ. See also POSÉ

The dancer: 1, places an extended foot on the ground; or, 2, steps out, in any direction.

POSITIONS. See ARMS, pp. 12–13; FEET; FOOT; HANDS; HEAD; LEG; also DIRECTIONS; OUVERTE

FIGURE 117   FIGURE 118

PREPARATION

Certain preparatory movements for difficult steps in which the dancer assembles himself before turning or jumping—i.e. sous-sus before TOUR EN L'AIR—are often referred to as preparation.

PRESSÉS. See GLISSADE

PROMENADE or PIVOT

1. The dancer turns steadily on the spot on one foot, moving the heel inch by inch: for example see ARABESQUE. 2. A dancer is taken round on the toe by her partner, who holds her waist or hands, in a position: for examples see ATTITUDE and ARABESQUE.

To-day the man may pull his partner backwards or forwards or even sideways on point while she maintains a pose on her toe.

PSYCHOLOGICAL BALLET

The word " psychological " first come to be used in ballet in connection with the works of Tudor, because he was the first choreographer to attempt to show not only what people did but why they did it, in accord with the current scientific investigations in this field. So far only a few ballets of Tudor's have attempted to present all the reasons and consequent events on the stage, but the application of this method can be admired in most of his works.

93

QUADRILLES, PREMIERE or DEUXIEME. See BALLERINA, PRIMA

QUARRÉ, EN or EN CARRÉ

Steps performed to describe a square on the stage: a formation often seen in " Checkmate."

RACCOURCI. See LEG, POSITIONS OF THE; RETIRÉ; FONDU

RAKE OF THE STAGE. See also CLASS (p. 33)

Many stages rise sharply as they go back, hence the terms "up-stage" and " down-stage "; this is now done for the benefit of the occupants of the stalls but was originally introduced by the magnificent theatrical designers of the 16th and 17th centuries who wished to exploit the then novel laws of perspective. This sharp inclination of the stage can be very upsetting to even the most adroit beginner.

RAMASSÉ. See SISSONE

RATS. See BALLERINA, PRIMA

RECULANT, EN. See DIRECTIONS

RÉGISSEUR-GÉNÉRALE

Strictly speaking, the term *régisseur-générale* means stage manager. However, this was the title given to the man who more than any-body else helped Diaghilev to steer his company through the various difficulties of twenty years. Therefore, since the career of Grigoriev (in many ways the most extraordinary personality ever associated with that extraordinary ballet company) the term *régisseur-générale* has come to mean a factotum whose all-seeing eye controls not only stage performance details, but also proper-ties, make-up and hair styles, costume details, choreographical points, and even, in the absence of the choreographer, takes rehearsals, and remounts ballets, as Grigoriev and his wife Tchernichova have done so successfully for the Royal Ballet and other companies.

REINS, TOUR DE. See JETÉ (p. 72)

RELEVÉ or MONTER. See also PIROUETTE ; RETIRÉ

The dancer raises the heel of the supporting foot (or feet) off the ground, generally straightening the supporting knee or knees.

A *relevé* with both feet together is similar to, but gives a much smoother appearance than, a SOUS-SUS; although many dancers are trained to give a very slight spring up when rising on to the toes in this manner. Such a spring does not increase the softness of the movement, but lessens the great strain otherwise put on the muscles of the leg.

Shortly after leaving her partner at the back of the stage, the female dancer of the pas de deux *in " Les Sylphides " runs to the front left-hand corner of the stage and performs a series of* relevés *on the left toe, with the other leg extended behind her, travelling diagonally backwards (not to be confused with* VOYAGÉ) *and bending her wrists.*

Relevés *on both feet with the legs opened to front and back are a feature of Summer's variation in " Cinderella " (Ashton).*

(*N.B.* Sometimes the term ÉLEVÉ is used in place of *relevé*, usually when the dancer rises once on to her toes, instead of repeating the movement several times.)

RELEVÉ PASSÉ. See RETIRÉ; *BATTEMENT RELEVÉ.* See CLASS (p. 35)

RENVERSÉ

The dancer sways his body from one side to the other as he turns, giving the impression that he is off balance. This movement is generally executed during a single turn—which may come at the end of a preliminary series of turns.

The two most common *renversés*, PAS DE BOURRÉE *renversé* EN DEHORS and PIROUETTE *renversé* EN DEDANS, are abbreviated to *renversé en dehors* and *renversé en dedans* respectively.

RÉPÉTITION. RÉPÉTITION GÉNÉRALE

Rehearsal. Final dress rehearsal.

RETIRÉ or *RACCOURCI.* See also CLASS (p. 36); LEG, POSITIONS OF THE; SOUBRESAUT: FONDU; PASSÉ

1. The dancer's foot is drawn up to touch the supporting leg, bending the knee (*retiré*). 2. An extended foot is similarly drawn in to the supporting leg (*raccourci*).

(*N.B.* It is common to use either *retiré* or *raccourci* to cover both 1 and 2.)

Retirés PASSÉS are sometimes called RELEVÉS *passés* or *relevés*.

When both legs are drawn up beneath a dancer in this manner during a jump, the jumping step is said to be *retiré*.

Changements retirés are a feature of the dances of Harlequin in " Carnaval " (p. 97, Figure 119).

RETOMBÉ. See SISSONE

RÉVÉRENCE

The elaborate bow or curtsey performed at the end of class by male and female dancers respectively. It is obviously a relic of the courtly origins of ballet.

REVOLTADE or *RIBOULDADE* or *RIVOLTADE*

From the Italian *rivoltare*, to turn over.

With the right leg raised high in front of him, the dancer springs and raises the left leg over the top of the right leg, leaning forward as his body turns. He lands facing the opposite direction on the left leg, the right leg raised behind him. The impression is given that the dancer places one leg in the air and then jumps over it.

While in the air the left leg can either remain straight, or bend so that the foot passes over the right knee, as in Figure 120.

The three jumps performed by the leading male dancer of " Les Patineurs" immediately before the end of his solo, as he travels diagonally backwards, are rivoltades (*Figure* 120).

REVOLUTION

Sometimes used to describe a number of turns executed by two or more dancers turning while linked together.

RÔLE, TOUR DE

When the soloists share a rôle this term is used. Not to be confused with understudy.

ROLLING

Most people stand naturally with most of the weight of the body either on the outside or the inside of their feet; dancers call the former rolling out and the latter rolling in. Some students attempt to roll in a direction the reverse of their natural one, either because they think this looks attractive or because their teacher tells them it is necessary. Those who have read the section on ARQUÉ will realise the wide differences there can be in the formation of human legs, and realise that the platform on which the dancer stands must obviously be built differently in each individual; the racks of unmended shoes in a shoemender's shop show how differently individuals wear down parts of the sole and heel according to the way in which they place their feet on the ground, despite the initial uniformity of the manufactured sole. Ballet shoes do not

—————— FIGURE 119   —————— FIGURE 120

offer any resistance to the foot placing itself on the ground, and as the essential part of any structure is a steady base, the way in which one's feet naturally grip the floor is obviously the best.

Any attempts to twist the ankle either outward or inward against the natural inclination of the foot will unsteady the dancer before he takes his first step, and he will ever after be struggling between what is natural and comfortable to him and what he has been taught to attempt. There are quite enough difficulties to overcome in ballet without adding another which contributes nothing to technique, is of doubtful beauty and has the additional drawback of unsteadying the foot and body. Presumably the attempt to counter the slight natural inclination of the foot comes from ignorance of the existence of *arqués* and *jarretés* and a consequent desire to make dancers try to be exactly alike.

ROMANTIC BALLET. See CLASSICAL BALLET

ROMANTIC DANCER. See CLASSICAL DANCER (p. 44)

RONDS DE JAMBE. See CLASS (p. 35) ; p. 54, Figures 59, 60, 62, 63; FOUETTÉ. *DOUBLÉ.* See GARGOUILLADE

ROOM, CORNERS OF; POINTS OF. See DIRECTIONS

ROSIN

A by-product of turpentine, rosin is used by dancers on the stage or in the studio to prevent slipping. In earlier times water was always used for this purpose : in the paintings of Degas the watering-can is frequently seen, and on the old photographs of the first performances of " Les Sylphides " in Paris the water tracks on the stage are clearly visible. Teachers such as Idzikowski used water, but in many instances today it is replaced by rosin, or detergent.

Rosin should only be used when it is really needed, that is on a very slippery stage. If it is constantly used, whether necessary or not, it is useless in an emergency, and too much rosin causes the dancer's shoes to squeak on the stage in pirouettes and other turning movements.

ROTATION. See FOUETTÉ (p. 67)

ROYALE. See ÉCHAPPÉ; ENTRECHAT

RUSSIAN METHOD. See METHOD

SALLE, AUTOUR DE LA. See MANÈGE, EN

SAUT

A jump in which the dancer springs off both feet and lands in the same position. The feet are not crossed as in SOUBRESAUT.

SAUTÉ

When added to the name of a step, the movement is then performed while jumping, i.e. RONDS DE JAMBE EN L'AIR *sautés*.

SENS. See DIRECTIONS (pp. 50–55)

SERPETTE or SICKLE FOOT

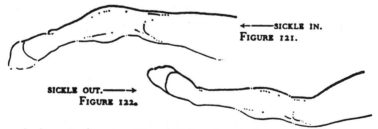

←———SICKLE IN.
FIGURE 121.

SICKLE OUT.———→
FIGURE 122.

A dancer's foot is said to sickle when it forms an angle to the straight line from hip to ankle, instead of carrying it straight on.

Excessive sickling breaks the line of the leg.

SERRÉ. See CLASS (p. 37); FERMÉ

SEUL, PAS. See PAS

SICKLE FOOT. See SERPETTE

SIDE PRACTICE. See CLASS (p. 33)

SISSONE or *SISOL* or *JETÉ FROM BOTH FEET.* See also TOUR EN L'AIR; FAILLI

The dancer, who is standing on both feet, springs in the air and lands on one foot.

When the dancer's movement is only in a vertical direction and he lands with the raised foot touching the other knee or ankle, the step is called *sissone* SIMPLE : if he travels during the course of the spring the *sissone* is called EN AVANT (forwards), DE COTÉ (sideways), or EN ARRIÈRE (backwards), and the movement is caused by the dancer pushing himself away from one leg which he stretches after himself. The legs may beat before opening, sometimes called FAUX ENTRECHAT CINQ or ENTRECHAT CINQ RAMASSÉ.

A DÉVELOPPÉ SAUTÉ (see Class, p. 38) is sometimes called either *sissone développé* or *sissone* OUVERTE.

In his second solo in the " Peasant " pas de deux from " Giselle," the male dancer performs a sissone *in the centre of the stage to his right (raising the left leg), a* sissone *to his left, a* SOUS-SUS *and a double turn in the air to the right, repeats the sequence to the other side, and then once more as above (p. 101, Figure 124).*

In her solo in Act 2 of " Swan Lake," the first two times Odette moves diagonally she performs two sissones *forward with the arms extended in front; she then takes two little steps forward and performs a* développé PASSÉ *to the back while extending the arms behind her.*

A *développé sauté* or *sissone* followed by a COUPÉ and an ASSEMBLÉ are frequently called *sissone* DOUBLÉE or *sissone* RETOMBÉE.

The male solo in the " Don Quixote " pas de deux (Petipa-Oboukhoff) begins with a series of successive sissones en avant passés battus en attitude *(Figure 125)*—COUPÉS—ASSEMBLÉS forward *(sissones doublées).* Another example from " Giselle " Act 2 will be found under *développé sauté (Class, page 38).*

SOUBRESAUT. See also ANGE, SAUT DE L'

A jump with the body erect, in which the legs cling together without changing.

A *soubresaut* RETIRÉ in which the dancer's legs are bent beneath him while jumping is often called GRAND *soubresaut.*

99

(*N.B. Soubresauts* are always performed from the 5th or 3rd positions, without changing the feet: if the feet change the step is called *changement de pieds*, and if the step is performed with the feet in 1st, 2nd or 4th positions it is called *saut.*)

Soubresauts retirés *with the feet together are a feature of the dance of the Fairy Godmother and the Four Seasons in Ashton's "Cinderella".*

Soubresaut POISSON or TEMPS DE *poisson* or *temps* COLLÉ or SAUT DE *poisson.*

The dancer performs a *soubresaut*, arching the back and bending the feet and head well back.

In the second diagonal of his solo, the male dancer of the "Blue Bird" pas de deux performs a series of three alternating soubresauts poisson (*Figure* 124) *and* ASSEMBLÉS PORTÉS BATTUS (*p.* 14, *Figure* 22).

SOUBRESAUT SUR LES POINTES or SOUS-SUS or TEMPS DE COU-DE-PIED or RELEVÉ

The dancer performs a *sous-sus* by springing on to the toes, generally travelling forward, and bringing the legs tightly together. *Swanilda runs on and performs a* sous-sus *before beginning her solo in Act 3 of" Coppélia."*

SOUS DESSOUS SOUS DESSUS. See BRISÉ VOLÉ

SOUTENU. See also ASSEMBLÉ; FONDU

A movement is sustained or performed slowly; sometimes used also to imply that the dancer will so control his high jumps that they have the smooth and steady appearance of a slow motion film.

SPLITS. See CLASS (p. 41); ÉCART, LE GRAND

SPOTTING

When practising turns the dancer leaves his head facing the front until the last possible moment and then quickly swivels it round to the front again. It is usual when starting a series of turns to fix the eyes in the direction in which one wishes to finish, and to return the eyes to that spot at the completion of every turn. This adds sharpness to the turn; however, it is not done for that reason but because it avoids giddiness, as the dancer only sees one side of the room on each turn instead of all four sides.

STEP. See POSER; PAS

STULCHIK. See ENLÈVEMENT (pp. 60–61, Figures 68, 69, 71)

SUJET, GRAND: PETIT. See BALLERINA, PRIMA

FIGURE 123   FIGURE 124   FIGURE 125

SUPPORTING LEG. See WORKING LEG

SYMPHONIC BALLET

Though ballets choreographed to the musical accompaniment of
symphonies are not unknown before the nineteen-thirties—for
example, in 1916 Gorsky created "Fifth Symphony" (Glazunov),
while over a century ago Deshayes made choreography to
Beethoven's Sixth—it was Leonide Massine with his "Les Présages" and "Choreartium" who initiated the movement known
today as "symphonic ballet." The thirties was a period which
saw the rise of high passions, politically speaking, so it was perhaps natural that symphonic ballet was discussed and argued over
no less passionately in the sphere of the dance theatre. Many
persons writing about ballet, though quite unmoved when
Fokine set a ballet to piano music of Chopin or to Rimsky-
Korsakov's "Schéhérazade," nearly burst a blood vessel when
Massine attempted to arrange choreography to the Brahms Fourth,

and the fact that the vast majority of the audience applauded " Choreartium " with fervour seemed to annoy them even more. Chief (or most vocal) of those against the use of "absolute" music for ballet was the ballet conductor/composer, Constant Lambert, who disparaged Massine's efforts in this field while praising Balanchine's story-ballets of that period. Despite the fact that nowadays George Balanchine pursues this almost out-worn form *ad nauseam* without a single word of protest from the musical purists, yet echoes of the Massine/symphonic ballet controversy still arise occasionally, as for example when " Les Présages " arrived in Holland twenty years after, upon which the old controversy revived for a week or two.

With symphonic ballet Massine set a new standard for abstract, serious dancing to abstract, serious music, and this new attitude to dancing (which has previously only been used either to tell a story or to display personalities and individual tricks in *divertissements*) completely altered the face of ballet in our time. The choreo-grapher himself has long since abandoned this type of work as the blind alley which Lambert declared it to be, though within its limits it can produce, as in " Choreartium " or " Symphonic Variations," a spectacle of dazzling beauty.

TAQUETÉ, TAQUETERIE

Steps performed on the tips of the toes in a sharp staccato manner. Steps performed in this manner are called *taqueterie*.

TEMPS DE POINTE

All steps performed on point, that is, on the tips of the toes.

TEMPS LEVÉ. See also TOUR EN L'AIR ; CABRIOLE

A hop off one foot while the other is held in a position.
The male dancer in " Les Sylphides " runs across the stage and commences his solo with three temps levé with the right leg raised in ARABESQUE, *which step is frequently repeated throughout the solo.*

Shortly after the entrance of the male dancer in " Le Spectre de la Rose " he makes a wide circle round the stage performing temps levé, step, step, *temps levé* (p. 105, Figure 126), step, step, *then four* temps levé *off alternate feet.*

TEMPS LEVÉ CHASSÉ or DEMI-CONTRETEMPS

Standing in fourth position with the weight over the front foot, and the back foot either completely on the ground, resting on the toe, or in the air, the dancer springs up and, on descending, slides the back leg through to the front (CHASSÉ PASSÉ). This can also be performed in reverse with the front foot moving through to the back (EN ARRIÈRE).

If a beat is added before sliding the leg through, the movement may be called *temps levé chassé* BATTU, DEMI-CONTRETEMPS *battu*, or CABRIOLE chassé.

(*N.B.* This step is sometimes confused with FAILLI, *q.v.*)

TEMPS LIÉ

Name sometimes given to a series of exercises mainly composed of sliding movements into the open positions, with stylised arm movements and body bends designed to improve balance and smoothness. These are generally improvised by the teacher, and sometimes replace *port de bras* and centre practice (see CLASS p. 41).

TEMPS PLANÉ. See ANGE, TEMPS DE L'; PLANÉ

TENDU. See CLASS (p. 34); LEG, POSITIONS OF THE

TERMINÉ

Indicates that a step is to be finished in a certain manner: for example PIROUETTE EN ARABESQUE *terminé* EN ATTITUDE.

TERRE, À or PAR TERRE

On the ground. A *terre à terre* dance is one with few jumps. Certain steps, for example GLISSADES, lose their quality if not performed *terre à terre*.

THROWING THE WEIGHT. See CLASS (pp. 41–42)

TIGHTS or MAILLOT

A close-fitting garment covering the dancer's body up to the waist or armpits. For practice dancers frequently wear footless tights.

TIRE-BOUCHON, EN. See LEG, POSITIONS OF THE

TIROIRS, FAIRE LES

Two or more opposite lines of dancers cross the stage passing each other and the re-cross, generally performing the same steps.
Shortly before Giselle's entrance in Act 2, the six lines of corps de ballet cross and re-cross the stage in this fashion.

TOE DANCING: TOE SHOES. See POINTE

TOMBÉ

From a position on a straight supporting leg, the dancer falls on
to the other leg, of which the knee remains bent at the conclusion
of the fall. The *tombé* is made either to the front (*en avant*), to
the side (*à la seconde*), or backwards (*en arrière*).

When the fall is carried through so that the supporting leg is
raised in a position at the conclusion of the *tombé*, the term *tombé*
EN ARABESQUE, EN ATTITUDE, and so forth, is used, in accordance
with the final position of the lifted leg.

TONNELET

The short wired skirt conventionally worn by the *danseur noble*
during the 18th century. These were reproduced by Bouchène
in his costume designs for Fokine's " Les Éléments," and by
Stevenson in his designs for Tudor's " Gallant Assembly."
Noverre considered them ludicrous and cumbersome and expresses
his disapproval strongly in the " Letters."

TOUR. See PIROUETTE; JETÉ (pp. 72, 75); RÔLE, TOUR DE

TOUR EN L'AIR (commonly called *DOUBLE TOUR* or *DOUBLE TURN*). See also SPOTTING

The dancer springs straight up and turns while in the air, once,
twice or rarely three times. *Tours en l'air* are commonly begun
with the feet together, the dancer springing up and turning in the
direction of the front foot, with his feet held closely together.
Tours en l'air are seldom executed from a position where the legs
begin wide apart, but to finish *tours en l'air* with the feet apart is not
uncommon. In either case the dancer keeps his legs together for
as long as possible, as it is much easier to balance in the air in such
a position. The legs may be beaten while turning.

In Russian character dancing the male dancer frequently performs
double *tours en l'air* with the knees bent and the feet tucked up
under the body, which makes this movement very spectacular.
*In the last movement of " Choreartium " the sixteen male dancers
performed* double tours *first in groups of four and then simultaneously.*

*This step is rarely performed by a girl, but the Polka in " Façade "
when created by Markova concluded with a double turn.*

FIGURE 126   FIGURE 127

A double turn is often preceded by a PIROUETTE EN DEHORS. *Albrecht concludes his solo in Act 2 of " Giselle " with two* CHASSÉS COUPÉS CHASSÉS (*Figure 127*), ASSEMBLÉ EN AVANT, double tour, *repeated three times diagonally forward; followed by a* pirouette en dehors *and a* double tour *after which he falls to the ground* (tour en l'air AVEC CHUTE ALLONGÉE).

TOUR EN L'AIR SUR LE COU-DE-PIED or RETIRÉ, also called TEMPS LEVÉ EN TOURNANT DEHORS, is far more difficult than the above *tour en l'air*, because in this turn the dancer draws one foot to the other ankle or knee as he springs, turning and landing in that position. This is in fact a *sissone simple en tournant*, as it starts from two feet and concludes on one, but it is commonly referred to as a *tour en l'air;* whereas *saut de basque, temps de flêche* and *jeté enveloppé* are always referred to by those names whether turns are added or not.

(*N.B.* Both kinds of *tours en l'air* can be commenced by the dancer bending his knees to the fullest extent before springing into the air this is particularly difficult and rare; this virtuoso movement occurs in " Dances at a Gathering ".

TOURNANT, EN

1. The dancer turns during the course of a step, for instance ASSEMBLÉ *en tournant*, PAS DE BOURRÉE COURU *en tournant*.

2. The dancer turns while a step is repeated, for example eight GLISSADES travelling in a circle, or four ENTRECHATS turning to a different side on each jump and thereby completing one turn.

TOURNE-HANCHE. See also TURN-OUT

A short-lived 18th century mechanical device intended to effect a turn-out by fixing the feet in a turned-out position in a box. As Noverre pointed out, this by no means fulfilled the purpose for which it was designed as it did not affect the hip joint but only turned-out the ankle and knee joints which had to bear the strain of the difference in turn-out at either extreme of the leg.

TOURNER. See MOVEMENT, CATEGORIES OF

TOURS, DEMI or DÉBOULÉS or PETITS TOURS or TOURS CHAINÉS or CHAINÉS DÉBOULÉS PIROUETTES. See also SPOTTING

These half turns make little effect unless they are performed in a series, well up on the toes, with the legs held closely together.

While appearing to keep the whole body rigid, the dancer, standing with his weight on the right leg, turns his back to the audience and steps on to the left foot. He then completes the turn stepping on to the right foot, and so on in a series travelling across the stage.

The movement looks most ungainly if the legs are allowed to separate: for this reason it is not common to turn the legs right out and in fact many dancers do not turn-out at all while performing this step.

Just before the curtain falls on "Les Patineurs" five of the leading dancers cross the stage diagonally performing demi-tours.

TRAVESTI, EN

A female dancer is appearing *en travesti* when dressed as a man, and—more rarely—a male dancer when dressed as a woman.

TURN-OUT OF THE HIPS or L'EN DEHORS
See also ROLLING; TOURNE-HANCHE

The principle of turned-out legs was first defined in Arbeau's "*Orchésographie*" (1588) and found practical application in the formulation of the five positions of the feet by Beauchamp at the end of the 17th century. The turn-out is merely a means to the end of greater flexibility and range of movement, and therefore is strictly adhered to in every ballet class, but not inevitably on the stage. The turn-out must not be made from the ankle, but should be the result of turning-out of the legs in the hip joints. If the student persists in trying to turn his feet further out than the construction of the hips will allow the entire leg to turn, he will automatically weaken both ankles and knees, which have to bear the strain of the difference in turn-out at each extreme of the leg.

While almost all ballet steps are performed turned out, there are some which the dancer performs turned in, including *pas de course; pas de valse; pas de bourree couru* when the feet do not cross (p. 23, Figure 29); *demi-tours;* while the supporting leg in *arabesque* is not turned out in relation to the hip.

TUTU

The conventional ballet skirt, either short and fluffy, or stretching to calf or ankle (JUPONNAGE). It is made of many layers of nylon or tarlatan, and was originally the under-skirt.

VALSE, PAS DE

Resembles a BALANCÉ but the feet do not cross, remaining close together and parallel.

Standing on the right foot the left heel is lowered to the ground; next the toe of the right takes the weight for a moment; finally the weight returns strongly to the left foot. The sequence may then be repeated to the other side.

VARIATION. See also ADAGE

Solo. As used in ballet, this word bears no relation to music where a variation is an elaboration of a previously stated theme.

VIDEO-TAPE See also NOTATION

An invaluable method—by far superior to film—of recording ballets. Its use has been pioneered with great success by Netherlands Dance Theatre.

VOLÉ. See BRISÉ VOLÉ ; ASSEMBLÉ

VOYAGÉ

When added to the name of a position, means that the dancer maintains that pose while travelling by a series of small swift hops on a bent leg, without stretching the supporting foot.

WARMING UP

A dancers' expression covering exercises (generally from BARRE) which they perform in the wings before going on to the stage. Before attempting difficult roles calling for technical feats and dexterity of execution, dancers invariably " warm-up " as a precaution against muscle strain and accident, just as athletes warm up and a singer will run through scales in the dressing-room before an operatic performance. " Warming-up " is a similar physical check to make certain that the limbs and muscles are pliable and ready for the strain about to be placed upon them. In cold climates dancers often wear more than one pair of woollen tights and then shake and pummel their legs to warm themselves before commencing even a *barre* in the wings or class.

WATERING CAN. See ROSIN

WORKING LEG, SUPPORTING LEG

These terms are used by teachers and dancers to differentiate between the functions of the dancer's legs when performing various steps. Their use is entirely logical when dealing with such steps as the *double ronds de jambes en l'air en dedans* performed three times on alternating feet by Odette at the beginning of her solo in Act 2 of " Swan Lake " (p. 36, *Figure* 39), since obviously the leg on which she is standing can only be the supporting leg, while the other leg describing *ronds de jambes en l'air* is equally obviously " working " harder than the other. The same is also true of the example immediately following (p. 36, illustrated by p. 39, *Figure* 41), even though the dancer is in the air : but when such a step as *brisé ballonné* or *brisé* (p. 25, *Figure* 31) is concerned, the conventional use of " working " and " supporting " leg becomes ridiculous, since the " working " leg—i.e. that which leaves the ground first—in this case does far less work than the " supporting " leg, which has to push off from the ground, beat the other calf, and then take the dancer's weight in *plié* before repeating the whole sequence again.

ZÉPHYR, PAS DE

A series of BATTEMENTS EN CLOCHE (p. 38) performed with a little jump, added when the moving leg reaches the height of the movement, either behind or in front. When a beat (CABRIOLE) is added at the highest point of the jump, the term used is *pas de zéphyr* BATTU.

INDEX

Page numbers in *italics* refer to illustrations